D1236492

1961 ▶ ——————— (Ended in failure)
Pallet kanban

1962 ▶
Kanban adopted company-wide
(machining, forging, body assembly, etc.)

1961 ▶
Red and blue card system
for ordering outside parts

1965 ▶
Kanban adopted for ordering
outside parts, 100% supply system;
began teaching Toyota system to affiliates

1959 ▶
Transfer system (in ⟶ in or in ⟶ out)

1973 ▶
Transfer system
(out ⟶ in)

1962 ▶
Main plant setups (15 minutes)

1971 ▶
Main office and
Motomachi setups
(3 minutes)

1963 ▶
Use of inter-writer; system
of autonomated selection of
parts adopted; information
indicator system adopted

1971 ▶
Body indication system
(Motomachi Crown line)

1963 ▶
Multi-process operation

1962 ▶
Full-work control of machines,
machine *baka-yoke*

1966 ▶
First autonomated line,
Kamigō plant

1961 ▶
Andon installed, Motomachi assembly plant

1971 ▶
Fixed-position stopping
system in assembly

D   U   C   T   I   O   N   L   E   V   E   L   I   N   G

Toyota Production System

Toyota Production System
Beyond Large-Scale Production

▼

Taiichi Ohno

Foreword by Norman Bodek

Productivity Press

Productivity Press
444 Park Avenue South, 7th flr
New York, NY 10016
Telephone: 212-686-5900
Fax: 212-686-5411
E-mail: info@productivitypress.com

Book and cover design by Bill Stanton
Printed and bound by Sheridan Books
Printed in the United States of America

Library of Congress Cataloging-in-Publication Data

Ōno, Taiichi, 1912-1990
    Toyota production system.

    Translation of: *Toyota seisan hōshiki.*
    Includes index.
    1. Production control. 2. Toyota Jidosha Kogyo
Kabushiki kaisha. I. Title.
TS157.05713   1988 629.2'34'0685   87-43172
ISBN 0-915299-14-3

08   07   25   24

Table of Contents

Publisher's Foreword

JUST AS WE have been recognizing the greatness of Mr. Shigeo Shingo, we also recognize the genius of Mr. Taiichi Ohno. It was Mr. Ohno who should be credited with the creation of the Toyota just-in-time production system.

I met Mr. Ohno in Japan at Toyoda Gōsei where he became chairman after retiring from Toyota Motors. Toyoda Gōsei is a Toyota subcontractor manufacturing steering wheels, automobile parts like rubber hoses and plastic dashboards, and other materials.

At our last meeting I asked him where Toyota was today in the improvement process. By now, the company must have reduced all work-in-process inventory — lowering the water level in the river to expose all the rocks, enabling them to chip away at all the problems.

"What is Toyota doing now?" I asked.

His answer was very simple.

"All we are doing is looking at the time line," he said, "from the moment the customer gives us an order to the point when we collect the cash. And we are reducing that time line by removing the non-value-added wastes."

Time Line

Order   Cash

├──┤

(reduce by removing non-value-added wastes)

Simple but brilliant. It gives a very clear focus to continuous improvement. Where we in the West would look immediately for some magic automatic miracle like computer integrated manufacturing (CIM), robotics, or advanced manufacturing techniques, the Japanese are simply reducing wastes. Of course, some wastes can be removed by acquiring new equipment but that should be done last — not first.

There is nothing very complex in the magic of Mr. Ohno's teachings. In fact, it is often confusing listening to him because he talks so simply, often just saying to look for and eliminate waste. We cannot believe that it is that simple — but it is true. Just reduce the time line by removing any wastes.

Mr. Ohno's simple tale told in the book is brilliant and should be read by managers everywhere. It is not just a tale of manufacturing, it is a tale of how to run a business successfully. Mr. Ohno went back and reviewed how Henry Ford ran his business. Henry Ford was able to mine iron ore on a Monday and, using that very same iron ore, produce a car coming off the assembly line on Thursday afternoon.

Henry Ford also focused on the total elimination of non-valued-added wastes. Mr. Ohno just simply updated Henry Ford. He reduced changeover times with the help of Mr. Shingo from days and hours to minutes and seconds. He eliminated job classifications to give workers flexibility.

In the past 10 years, I have visited hundreds of manufacturing plants in Japan and the United States. I never see a Japanese worker just watching a machine. In the United States, it is the reverse — I have never visited an American plant without seeing a worker just watching a machine. I will never forget walking through a fiber optics cable manufacturing operation and watching a young man just looking at a glass extrusion machine.

All he did was watch the glass and the dials waiting for the glass to break or be out of tolerance. I could not believe the waste and the lack of respect management had for that human being. Manufacturing must be both efficient and also have respect for the person running the machine.

The world owes a great deal to Mr. Taiichi Ohno. He has shown us how to manufacture more efficiently, reduce costs, produce greater quality, and also take an important look at how we as people work in a factory.

A Japanese factory is far from perfect. Toyota plants, at least the ones I have seen, are as dirty if not dirtier than many American plants I have visited. But a change is happening. Respect for humanity in the manufacturing process is becoming a reality and Mr. Ohno is one of the world's leaders in this area.

While most companies focused on stimulating sales, Mr. Ohno believed just-in-time was a manufacturing advantage for Toyota. And for many years, he would not allow anything to be recorded about it. He claimed it was because improvement is never-ending — and by writing it down, the process would become crystallized. But I think he also feared Americans would discover this powerful tool and use it against the Japanese.

Just-in-time is much more than an inventory reduction system. It is much more that reducing changeover times. It is much more than using *kanban* or *jidoka*. It is much more than modernizing the factory. It is, in a sense, like Mr. Ohno says: *making a factory operate for the company just like the human body operates for an individual.* The autonomic nervous system responds even when we are asleep. The human body functions in good health when it is properly cared for, fed and watered correctly, exercised frequently, and treated with respect.

It is only when a problem arises that we become conscious of our bodies. Then we respond by making corrections. The same thing happens in a factory. We should have a system in a factory that automatically responds when problems occur.

You should all enjoy spending a few moments with Mr. Ohno and thinking about how you might improve your own manufacturing companies and each other, improve yourself, and help make a better world for us all.

I am extremely grateful to be able as a company to bring Mr. Ohno's classic book on the Toyota production system to the English reader. I want to acknowledge the contributions of Mr. Yuzuru Kawashima, proprietor, and Mr. Katsuyoshi Saito, deputy manager, of Diamond Inc., the original Japanese publisher, for granting us the rights to translate and publish this work.

I also thank those who helped create this English version — the book's editor, Cheryl Berling Rosen; Connie Dyer, clarifier of numerous content questions; Andrew P. Dillon,

clarifier of numerous translation questions; Patricia Slote and
Esmé McTighe, production coordinators; Bill Stanton, book
and cover designer; and, last but not least, the staff of Rudra
Press, our faithful friends, typesetters, and artists.

Finally, I wish to express my indebtedness to the author,
who has inspired so many of us in our quest for improving the
quality and productivity of today's workplace.

Norman Bodek
Chairman, Productivity, Inc.

Preface to the English Edition

THE TOYOTA PRODUCTION system, under the name of a *kanban* or a just-in-time system, has become the topic of much conversation in many workplaces and offices. It has been studied and introduced into workplaces regardless of industrial type, scale, and even national boundaries. And, indeed, this is a happy occurrence.

The Toyota production system evolved out of need. Certain restrictions in the marketplace required the production of small quantities of many varieties under conditions of low demand, a fate the Japanese automobile industry had faced in the postwar period. These restrictions served as a touchstone to test whether Japanese car manufacturers could establish themselves and survive in competition with the mass production and mass sales systems of an industry already established in Europe and the United States.

The most important objective of the Toyota system has been to increase production efficiency by consistently and thoroughly eliminating waste. This concept and the equally important respect for humanity that has passed down from the venerable Toyoda Sakichi (1867-1930), founder of the company and master of inventions, to his son Toyoda Kiichirō (1894-1952), Toyota Motor Company's first president and father of the Japanese passenger car, are the foundation of the Toyota production system.

The Toyota production system was conceived and its implementation begun soon after World War II. But it did not begin to attract the attention of Japanese industry until the first oil crisis in the fall of 1973. Japanese managers, accustomed to inflation and a high growth rate, were suddenly confronted with zero growth and forced to handle production decreases. It was during this economic emergency that they first noticed the results Toyota was achieving with its relentless pursuit of the elimination of waste. They then began to tackle the problem of introducing the system into their own workplaces.

The world has already changed from a time when industry could sell everything it produced to an affluent society where material needs are routinely met. Social values have changed. We are now unable to sell our products unless we think ourselves into the very hearts of our customers, each of whom has different concepts and tastes. Today, the industrial world has been forced to master in earnest the multi-kind, small-quantity production system.

The starting concept of the Toyota production system was, as I have emphasized several times, a thorough elimination of waste. In fact, the closer we came to this goal, the clearer became the picture of individual human beings with distinct personalities. There is no real substance to that abstract mass we call "the public." We discovered that industry has to accept orders from each customer and make products that differ according to individual requirements.

All kinds of wastes occur when we try to produce the same product in large, homogeneous quantities. In the end, costs rise. It is much more economical to make each item one at a time. The former method is the Ford production system and the latter is the Toyota production system.

I have no intention of criticizing Henry Ford (1863-1947). Rather, I am critical of Ford's successors who have suffered from excessive dependence on the authority of the Ford system precisely because it has been so powerful and created such wonders of industrial productivity. However, times change. Manufacturers and workplaces can no longer base production on desk-top planning alone and then distribute, or *push*, their products onto the market. It has become a matter of course for customers, or users, each with a different value system, to stand in the frontline of the marketplace and, so to speak, *pull* the goods they need, in the amount and at the time they need them.

The Toyota production system, however, is not just a production system. I am confident it will reveal its strength as a management system adapted to today's era of global markets and high-level computerized information systems.

I would appreciate receiving the criticisms, corrections, and frank opinions of my readers.

Taiichi Ohno
June 1987

A Comment on This Book

IN COUNTRIES AROUND the world, people are studying production methods. In Japan, the Toyota production system was developed some 30 years ago by Mr. Taiichi Ohno, presently vice president of the Toyota Motor Company. This revolutionary method is showing tremendous results today and will continue to evolve in the future.

The multi-step production system characteristic of many production processes involves *push* and *pull* methods. In the widely used push method, planned production quantity is determined by demand predictions and inventory on hand; succeeding production periods are determined from standard information prepared at certain times for each step; the product is then produced in sequence starting from step one. In the pull method, the final process withdraws the required quantities from the preceding process at a certain time, and this procedure is repeated in reverse order up through all the earlier processes. Each method has merits and shortcomings. Choosing one or the other and applying it effectively depends on the philosophy and practical creativity of managers and supervisors.

The Toyota production system is a pull method. To understand its tremendous success, one has to grasp the philosophy behind it without being sidetracked by particular aspects of the system, such as *kanban*. Kanban are instructions enclosed in clear plastic that at a glance communicate information needed at the work station. If the kanban system is introduced without being part of a total philosophy, however, I feel problems will ensue. The system did not happen overnight but through a series of innovations — a method developed over 30 years to improve overall efficiency and to enhance the work environment.

For this reason, I think it benefits the industrial world that Mr. Ohno, the man most responsible for the Toyota production system, has written this book to describe his philosophy and ideas for reform.

Mr. Ohno is a determined man with some very special skills. He has always challenged existing concepts and been able to conceive of and apply improvements that are both accurate and swift. People who can do this are rare, and I have learned much from observing him and listening to his theories.

Theories alone, however, may not improve the character of a business or increase productivity. For this reason, I recommend this book not only to those associated with production and manufacturing, but to any manager or supervisor. By reading this book and then using creativity and imagination to apply the theories, improvement should result even in companies unlike Toyota.

Muramatsu Rintarō
Faculty of Science and Engineering
Waseda University

A Note on Japanese Names

IN JAPAN, THE family name appears first. Thus, the famed inventor of the Toyota production system is known in Japan as Ōno Taiichi, and not Taiichi Ohno as usually written in the West.

In Productivity Press books we try to follow the Japanese practice of placing the surname first, in part, to make the representation of Japanese names uniform but primarily out of common courtesy. The reader therefore will find members of the Toyoda family referred to as Toyoda Sakichi, Toyoda Kiichirō, Toyoda Eiji, and so forth. However, when a person such as Taiichi Ohno is frequently referred to in other Western publications and the media in the Western manner, we refer to him or her likewise.

Also, when romanizing Japanese characters, a macron is used over a long vowel in all Japanese words except for well-known place names (Kyoto, Tokyo), words that have entered the English language (shogun, daimyo), and individual's names in which customarily the macron is replaced by an *h* (Ohno, not Ōno).

Toyota Production System

1

▼

Starting from Need

The Oil Crisis Opened Our Eyes

THE OIL CRISIS in the fall of 1973, followed by a recession, affected government, business, and society the world over. By 1974, Japan's economy had collapsed to a state of zero growth and many companies were suffering.

But at the Toyota Motor Company, although profits suffered, greater earnings were sustained in 1975, 1976, and 1977 than at other companies. The widening gap between it and other companies made people wonder what was happening at Toyota.

Prior to the oil crisis, when I talked to people about Toyota's manufacturing technology and production system, I found little interest. When rapid growth stopped, however, it became very obvious that a business could not be profitable using the conventional American mass production system that had worked so well for so long.

Times had changed. Initially, following World War II, no one imagined that the number of cars produced would increase to today's level. For decades, America had cut costs by mass- producing fewer types of cars. It was an American work style — but not a Japanese one. Our problem was how to cut costs while producing small numbers of many types of cars.

Then, during the 15-year period beginning in 1959-1960, Japan experienced unusually rapid economic growth. As a result, mass production, American style, was still used effectively in many areas.

We kept reminding ourselves, however, that careless imitation of the American system could be dangerous. Making many models in small numbers cheaply — wasn't this something we could develop? And we kept thinking that a Japanese production system like this might even surpass the conventional mass production system. Thus, the principal objective of the Toyota production system was to produce many models in small quantities.

▸ Slow Growth Is Scary

In the periods of high growth before the oil crisis, the usual business cycle consisted of two or three years of prosperity with, at most, six months of recession. At times, prosperity lasted longer than three years.

Slow growth, however, reverses this cycle. An annual economic growth rate of 6 to 10 percent lasts at most six months to one year, with the next two or three years realizing little or no growth or even negative growth.

Generally, Japanese industry has been accustomed to an era of "if you make it, you can sell it," and the automobile industry is no exception. I am afraid that, because of this, many business managers aim for quantity.

In the automobile industry, the Maxcy-Silberston[1] curve has been used frequently. According to this principle of mass production, although there are limits to the extent of cost reduction, the cost of an automobile decreases drastically in proportion to the increase in quantities produced. This was proved thoroughly in the era of high growth and the principle has become embedded in the minds of people in the automotive industry.

In today's slow-growth era, however, we must downplay the merits of mass production as soon as possible. Today, a production system aimed at increasing lot sizes (for example, operating a die press to punch out as many units as possible within a given time period) is not practical. Besides creating all kinds of waste, such a production system is no longer appropriate for our needs.

► "Catch Up with America"

Imitating America is not always bad. We have learned a lot from the U.S. automobile empire. America has generated wonderful production management techniques, business management techniques such as quality control (QC) and total quality control (TQC), and industrial engineering (IE) methods. Japan imported these ideas and put them into practice. The Japanese should never forget that these techniques were born in America and generated by American efforts.

August 15, 1945, was the day Japan lost the war; it also marked a new beginning for Toyota. Toyoda Kiichirō (1894–1952), then president of the Toyota Motor Company,[2] said, "Catch up with America in three years. Otherwise, the automobile industry of Japan will not survive." To accomplish this mission, we had to know America and learn American ways.

In 1937, I was working in the weaving plant of Toyoda Spinning and Weaving. Once I heard a man say that a German worker could produce three times as much as a Japanese worker. The ratio between German and American workers was 1-to-3. This made the ratio between Japanese and American work forces 1-to-9. I still remember my surprise at hearing that it took nine Japanese to do the job of one American.

Had Japanese productivity increased at all during the war? President Toyoda was saying that we should catch up in three years, but it would be very difficult to raise productivity by eight or nine times in such a time period. It meant that a job then being done by 100 workers had to be done by 10 workers.

Furthermore, the figure of one-eighth or one-ninth was an average value. If we compared the automobile industry, one of America's most advanced industries, the ratio would have been much different. But could an American really exert ten times more physical effort? Surely, Japanese people were wasting something. If we could eliminate the waste, productivity should rise by a factor of ten. This idea marked the start of the present Toyota production system.

▸ Just-In-Time

The basis of the Toyota production system is the absolute elimination of waste. The two pillars needed to support the system are:

- *just-in-time*
- *autonomation*, or automation with a human touch.

Just-in-time means that, in a flow process, the right parts needed in assembly reach the assembly line at the time they are needed and only in the amount needed. A company establishing this flow throughout can approach zero inventory.

From the standpoint of production management, this is an ideal state. However, with a product made of thousands of parts, like the automobile, the number of processes involved is enormous. Obviously, it is extremely difficult to apply just-in-time to the production plan of every process in an orderly way.

An upset in prediction, a mistake in the paperwork, defective products and rework, trouble with the equipment, absenteeism — the problems are countless. A problem early in the process always results in a defective product later in the process. This will stop the production line or change a plan whether you like it or not.

By disregarding such situations and only considering the production plan for each process, we would produce parts without regard to later processes. Waste would result — defective parts on one hand, huge inventories of parts not needed immediately on the other. This reduces both productivity and profitability.

Even worse, there would be no distinction between normal and abnormal states on each assembly line. When there is a delay in rectifying an abnormal state, too many workers would make too many parts, a situation not quickly corrected.

Therefore, to produce using just-in-time so that each process receives the exact item needed, when it is needed, and in the quantity needed, conventional management methods do not work well.

► Using a Common-Sense Idea

I am fond of thinking about a problem over and over. I kept thinking about how to supply the number of parts needed just-in-time. The flow of production is the transfer of materials. The conventional way was to supply materials from an earlier process to a later process. So, I tried thinking about the transfer of materials in the reverse direction.

In automobile production, material is machined into a part, the part is then assembled with others into a unit part, and this flows toward the final assembly line. The material progresses from the earlier processes toward the later ones, forming the body of the car.

Let's look at this production flow in reverse: a later process goes to an earlier process to pick up only the right part in the quantity needed at the exact time needed. In this case, wouldn't it be logical for the earlier process to make only the number of parts withdrawn? As far as communication between the many processes is concerned, wouldn't it be sufficient to clearly indicate what and how many are needed?

We will call this means of indication *kanban* (sign board) and circulate it between each of the processes to control the amount of production — that is, the amount needed. This was the beginning of the idea.

We experimented with this and finally decided on a system. The final assembly line is taken as the starting point. On this basis, the production plan, indicating the desired types of cars with their quantity and due date, goes to the final assembly line. Then the method of transferring the materials is reversed. To supply parts used in assembly, a later process goes to an earlier process to withdraw only the number of parts needed when they are needed. In this reverse way, the manufacturing process goes from finished product back to the earliest materials-forming department. Every link in the just-in-time chain is connected and synchronized. By this, the management work force is also reduced drastically. And kanban is the means used for conveying information about picking up or receiving the production order.

Kanban will be described later in detail. Here, I want the reader to understand the basic posture of the Toyota production system. The system is supported by the just-in-time system, already discussed, and autonomation, described in the next section. The kanban method is the means by which the Toyota production system moves smoothly.

▸ Give the Machine Intelligence

The other pillar of the Toyota production system is called autonomation — not to be confused with simple automation. It is also known as automation with a human touch.

Many machines operate by themselves once the switch is turned on. Today's machines have such high performance capabilities, however, that a small abnormality, such as a piece of scrap falling into the machine, can damage it in some way. The dies or taps break, for instance. When this happens, tens and soon hundreds of defective parts are produced and quickly pile up. With an automated machine of this type, mass production of defective products cannot be prevented. There is no built-in automatic checking system against such mishaps.

This is why Toyota emphasizes autonomation — machines that can prevent such problems "autonomously" — over simple automation. The idea originated with the invention of an auto-activated weaving machine by Toyoda Sakichi (1867-1930), founder of the Toyota Motor Company.

The loom stopped instantly if any one of the warp or weft threads broke. Because a device that could distinguish between normal and abnormal conditions was built into the machine, defective products were not produced.

At Toyota, a machine automated with a human touch is one that is attached to an automatic stopping device. In all Toyota plants, most machines, new or old, are equipped with such devices as well as various safety devices, fixed-position stopping, the full-work system, and *baka-yoke* foolproofing systems to prevent defective products (see the glossary for further explanation). In this way, human intelligence, or a human touch, is given to the machines.

Autonomation changes the meaning of management as well. An operator is not needed while the machine is working normally. Only when the machine stops because of an abnormal situation does it get human attention. As a result, one worker can attend several machines, making it possible to reduce the number of operators and increase production efficiency.

Looking at this another way, abnormalities will never disappear if a worker always attends to a machine and stands in for it when an abnormality does occur. An old Japanese saying mentions hiding an offensively smelly object by covering it up. If materials or machines are repaired without the managing supervisor's being made aware of it, improvement will never be achieved and costs will never be reduced.

Stopping the machine when there is trouble forces awareness on everyone. When the problem is clearly understood, improvement is possible. Expanding this thought, we establish a rule that even in a manually operated production line, the workers themselves should push the stop button to halt production if any abnormality appears.

In a product like the automobile, safety must always be of primary importance. Therefore, on any machine on any production line in any plant, distinctions between normal and abnormal operations must be clear and countermeasures always taken to prevent recurrence. This is why I made autonomation the other pillar of the Toyota production system.

► The Power of Individual Skill and Teamwork

Implementing autonomation is up to the managers and supervisors of each production area. The key is to give human intelligence to the machine and, at the same time, to adapt the simple movement of the human operator to the autonomous machines.

What is the relationship between just-in-time and automation with a human touch, the two pillars of the Toyota production system? Using the analogy of a baseball team, autonomation corresponds to the skill and talent of individual players while just-in-time is the teamwork involved in reaching an agreed-upon objective.

For example, a player in the outfield has nothing to do as long as the pitcher has no problems. But a problem — the opposing batter getting a hit, for example — activates the outfielder who catches the ball and throws it to the baseman "just in time" to put the runner out.

Managers and supervisors in a manufacturing plant are like the team manager and the batting, base, and field coaches. A strong baseball team has mastered the plays; the players can meet any situation with coordinated action. In manufacturing, the production team that has mastered the just-in-time system is exactly like a baseball team that plays well together.

Autonomation, on the other hand, performs a dual role. It eliminates overproduction, an important waste in manufacturing, and prevents the production of defective products. To accomplish this, standard work procedures, corresponding to each player's ability, must be adhered to at all times. When abnormalities arise — that is, when a player's ability cannot be brought out — special instruction must be given to bring the player back to normal. This is an important duty of the coach.

In the autonomated system, visual control, or "management by sight," can help bring production weaknesses (in each player, that is) to the surface. This allows us then to take measures to strengthen the players involved.

A championship team combines good teamwork with individual skill. Likewise, a production line where just-in-time and automation with a human touch work together is stronger than other lines. Its power is in the synergy of these two factors.

▸ Cost Reduction Is the Goal

Frequently we use the word "efficiency" when talking about production, management, and business. "Efficiency," in modern industry and business in general, means cost reduction.

At Toyota, as in all manufacturing industries, profit can be obtained only by reducing costs. When we apply the cost principle *selling price = profit + actual cost*, we make the consumer responsible for every cost. This principle has no place in today's competitive automobile industry.

Our products are scrutinized by cool-headed consumers in free, competitive markets where the manufacturing cost of a product is of no consequence. The question is whether or not the product is of value to the buyer. If a high price is set because of the manufacturer's cost, consumers will simply turn away.

Cost reduction must be the goal of consumer products manufacturers trying to survive in today's marketplace. During a period of high economic growth, any manufacturer can achieve lower costs with higher production. But in today's low-growth period, to achieve any form of cost reduction is difficult.

There is no magic method. Rather, a total management system is needed that develops human ability to its fullest capacity to best enhance creativity and fruitfulness, to utilize facilities and machines well, and to eliminate all waste.

The Toyota production system, with its two pillars advocating the absolute elimination of waste, was born in Japan out of necessity. Today, in an era of slow economic growth worldwide, this production system represents a concept in management that will work for any type of business.

▶ The Illusion of Japanese Industry

After World War II, when Toyoda Kiichirō, father of Japanese car production, advocated catching up with America in three years, this became Toyota's goal. Because the goal was clear, activity at Toyota became focused and vigorous.

My job until 1943 was in textiles, not automobiles; this was an advantage. In fact, the idea of automation with a human touch was obtained from the auto-activated looms of Toyoda Sakichi's textile plant. When I moved to automobile production, although I was new, I could spot its merits and shortcomings in comparison to the textile plant.

During postwar rehabilitation, Japan's automobile industry had a rough time. Domestic production for 1949 was 25,622 trucks and only 1,008 passenger cars. Insignificant as domestic production seemed, Toyota's production plant was filled with eager people trying to do something. President Toyoda's words "Catch up with America" generated this spirit.

In 1947, I was in charge of the No. 2 manufacturing machine shop at the present main office plant in Toyota City, then called the Koromo plant. To catch up with America, I thought of having one operator care for many machines and also different types of machines rather than one person per machine. Therefore, the first step was to establish a flow system in the machine shop.

In American as well as in most Japanese machine shops, a lathe operator, for example, operates only lathes. In many plant layouts, as many as 50 or 100 lathes are in one location. When machining is completed, the items are collected and taken to the subsequent drilling process. With that finished, the items then go to the milling process.

In the United States, there is a union for each job function with many unions in each company. Lathe operators are allowed to operate only lathes. A drilling job must be taken to a drilling operator. And because the operators are single-skilled, a welding job required at the lathe section cannot be done there but must be taken to a welding operator. As a consequence, there are a large number of people and machines. For American industries to achieve cost reduction under such conditions, mass production is the only answer.

When large quantities are produced, the labor cost per car and depreciation burden are reduced. This requires high-performance, high-speed machines that are both large and expensive.

This type of production is a planned mass production system in which each process makes many parts and forwards them to the next process. This method naturally generates an abundance of waste. From the time it acquired this American system until the 1973 oil crisis, Japan had the illusion that this system fit their needs.

▸ Establishing a Production Flow

It is never easy to break the machine-shop tradition in which operators are fixed to jobs, for example, lathe operators to lathe work and welders to welding work. It worked in Japan only because we were willing to do it. The Toyota production system began when I challenged the old system.

With the outbreak of the Korean War in June 1950, Japanese industry recovered its vigor. Riding this wave of growth, the automobile industry also expanded. At Toyota, it was a busy and hectic year, beginning in April with a three-month labor dispute over manpower reduction, followed by President Toyoda Kiichirō's assuming responsibility for the strike and resigning. After this, the Korean War broke out.

Although there were special wartime demands, we were far from mass production. We were still producing small quantities of many models.

At this time, I was manager of the machine shop at the Koromo plant. As an experiment, I arranged the various machines in the sequence of machining processes. This was a radical change from the conventional system in which a large quantity of the same part was machined in one process and then forwarded to the next process.

In 1947, we arranged machines in parallel lines or in an L-shape and tried having one worker operate three or four machines along the processing route. We encountered strong resistance among the production workers, however, even though there was no increase in work or hours. Our craftsmen did not like the new arrangement requiring them to function as multi-skilled operators. They did not like changing from "one operator, one machine" to a system of "one operator, many machines in different processes."

Their resistance was understandable. Furthermore, our efforts revealed various problems. For example, a machine must be set up to stop when machining is finished; sometimes there were so many adjustments that an unskilled operator found the job difficult to handle.

As these problems became clearer, they showed me the direction to continue moving in. Although young and eager to push, I decided not to press for quick, drastic changes, but to be patient.

▸ Production Leveling

In business, nothing is more pleasing than customer orders. With the labor dispute over and the special demands of the Korean War beginning, a lively tension filled the production plant. How would we handle the demand for trucks? People in the production plant were frantic.

There was a shortage of everything from crude materials to parts. We could not get things in the quantity or at the time needed. Our parts suppliers were also short on equipment and manpower.

Because Toyota made chassis, when many parts did not arrive on time or in the right amounts, assembly work was delayed. For this reason, we could not do assembly during the first half of the month. We were forced to gather the parts that were arriving intermittently and irregularly and do the assembly work at the end of the month. Like the old song *"dekansho"* that tells of sleeping half the year, this was *dekansho* production and the approach nearly did us in.

If a part is needed at the rate of 1,000 per month, we should make 40 parts a day for 25 days. Furthermore, we should spread production evenly throughout the workday. If the workday is 480 minutes, we should average one piece every 12 minutes. This idea later developed into production leveling.

Establishing (1) a production flow and (2) a way to maintain a constant supply of raw materials from outside for parts to be machined was the way the Toyota, or Japanese, production system should be operated. Our minds were filled with ideas.

Because there were shortages of everything, we must have thought it all right to increase manpower and machines to produce and store items. At the time, we were making no more than 1,000 to 2,000 cars a month, and keeping a one-month inventory in each process. Except for needing a large warehouse, this did not seem too big a burden. We did foresee a big problem, however, if and when production increased.

To avoid this potential problem, we looked for ways to level all production. We wanted to get away from having to produce everything around the end of the month, so we started by looking inside Toyota itself. Then, when outside suppliers were needed, we first listened to their needs and then asked them to cooperate in helping us achieve leveled production. Depending on the situation, we discussed the supplier's cooperation in terms of manpower, materials, and money.

▶ In the Beginning, There Was Need

So far, I have described, in sequence, the fundamental principles of the Toyota production system and its basic structure. I would like to emphasize that it was realized because there were always clear purposes and needs.

I strongly believe that "necessity is the mother of invention." Even today, improvements at Toyota plants are made based on need. The key to progress in production improvement, I feel, is letting the plant people feel the need.

Even my own efforts to build the Toyota production system block by block were also based on the strong need to discover a new production method that would eliminate waste and help us catch up with America in three years.

For example, the idea of a later process going to an earlier process to pick up materials resulted from the following circumstance. In the conventional system, an earlier process forwarded products to a later process continuously regardless of the production requirements of that process. Mountains of parts, therefore, might pile up at the later process. At that point, workers spent their time looking for storage space and hunting for parts instead of making progress in the most important part of their jobs — production.

Somehow this waste had to be eliminated and it meant immediately stopping the automatic forwarding of parts from earlier processes. This strong need made us change our method.

Rearranging the machines on the floor to establish a production flow eliminated the waste of storing parts. It also helped us achieve the "one operator, many processes" system and increased production efficiency two and three times.

I already mentioned that in America this system could not

be implemented easily. It was possible in Japan because we lacked function-oriented unions like those in Europe and the United States. Consequently, the transition from the single- to the multi-skilled operator went relatively smoothly, although there was initial resistance from the craftsmen. This does not mean, however, that Japanese unions are weaker than their American and European counterparts. Much of the difference lies in history and culture.

Some say that trade unions in Japan represent a vertically divided society lacking mobility while function-oriented unions of Europe and America exemplify laterally divided societies with greater mobility. Is this actually so? I don't think so.

In the American system, a lathe operator is always a lathe operator and a welder is a welder to the end. In the Japanese system, an operator has a broad spectrum of skills. He can operate a lathe, handle a drilling machine, and also run a milling machine. He can even perform welding. Who is to say which system is better? Since many of the differences come from the history and culture of the two countries, we should look for the merits in both.

In the Japanese system, operators acquire a broad spectrum of production skills that I call manufacturing skills and participate in building up a total system in the production plant. In this way, the individual can find value in working.

Needs and opportunities are always there. We just have to drive ourselves to find the practical ones. What are the essential needs of business under slow growth conditions? In other words, how can we raise productivity when the production quantity is not increasing?

▶ A Revolution in Consciousness Is Indispensable

There is no waste in business more terrible than overproduction. Why does it occur?

We naturally feel more secure with a considerable amount of inventory. Before, during, and after World War II, buying and hoarding were natural behaviors. Even in this more af-fluent time, people bought up tissue paper and detergent when the oil crisis came.

We could say this is the response of a farming society. Our ancestors grew rice for subsistence and stored it in preparation for times of natural disaster. From our experience during the oil crisis, we learned that our basic nature has not changed much.

Modern industry also seems stuck in this way of thinking. A person in business may feel uneasy about survival in this competitive society without keeping some inventories of raw materials, work-in-process, and products.

This type of hoarding, however, is no longer practical. In-dustrial society must develop the courage, or rather the com-mon sense, to procure only what is needed when it is needed and in the amount needed.

This requires what I call a revolution in consciousness, a change of attitude and viewpoint by business people. In a period of slow growth, holding a large inventory causes the waste of overproduction. It also leads to an inventory of defec-tives, which is a serious business loss. We must understand these situations in-depth before we can achieve a revolution in consciousness.

2

▼

Evolution of the Toyota Production System

Repeating *Why* Five Times

WHEN CONFRONTED WITH a problem, have you ever stopped and asked *why* five times? It is difficult to do even though it sounds easy. For example, suppose a machine stopped functioning:

1. *Why* did the machine stop?
   There was an overload and the fuse blew.
2. *Why* was there an overload?
   The bearing was not sufficiently lubricated.
3. *Why* was it not lubricated sufficiently?
   The lubrication pump was not pumping sufficiently.
4. *Why* was it not pumping sufficiently?
   The shaft of the pump was worn and rattling.
5. *Why* was the shaft worn out?
   There was no strainer attached and metal scrap got in.

Repeating *why* five times, like this, can help uncover the root problem and correct it. If this procedure were not carried through, one might simply replace the fuse or the pump shaft. In that case, the problem would recur within a few months.

To tell the truth, the Toyota production system has been built on the practice and evolution of this scientific approach. By asking *why* five times and answering it each time, we can get to the real cause of the problem, which is often hidden behind more obvious symptoms.

"Why can one person at Toyota Motor Company operate only one machine, while at the Toyoda textile plant one young woman oversees 40 to 50 automatic looms?"

By starting with this question, we obtained the answer "The machines at Toyota are not set up to stop when machining is completed." From this, automation with a human touch developed.

To the question "Why can't we make this part using just-in-time?" came the answer "The earlier process makes them so quickly we don't know how many are made per minute." From this, the idea of production leveling developed.

The first answer to the question "Why are we making too many parts?" was "Because there is no way to hold down or prevent overproduction." This led to the idea of visual control which then led to the idea of kanban.

It was stated in the previous chapter that the Toyota production system is based fundamentally on the absolute elimination of waste. Why is waste generated in the first place? With this question, we are actually asking the meaning of profit, which is the condition for a business's continued existence. At the same time, we are asking why people work.

In a production plant operation, data are highly regarded — but I consider facts to be even more important. When a problem arises, if our search for the cause is not thorough, the actions taken can be out of focus. This is why we repeatedly ask *why*. This is the scientific basis of the Toyota system.

▸ Complete Analysis of Waste

When thinking about the absolute elimination of waste, keep the following two points in mind:

1. Improving efficiency makes sense only when it is tied to cost reduction. To achieve this, we have to start producing only the things we need using minimum manpower.

2. Look at the efficiency of each operator and of each line. Then look at the operators as a group, and then at the efficiency of the entire plant (all the lines). Efficiency must be improved at each step and, at the same time, for the plant as a whole.

For example, throughout the 1950 labor dispute over manpower reduction and the ensuing business boom of the Korean War, Toyota struggled with the problem of how to increase production without increasing manpower. As one of the production plant managers, I put my ideas to work in the following ways.

Let's say, for instance, one production line has 10 workers and makes 100 products per day. This means the line capacity is 100 pieces per day and the productivity per person is 10 pieces per day. Observing the line and workers in further detail, however, we notice overproduction, workers waiting, and other unnecessary movements depending on the time of day.

Suppose we improved the situation and reduced manpower by two workers. The fact that 8 workers could produce 100 pieces daily suggests that we can make 125 pieces a day, increasing efficiency without reducing manpower. Actually, however, the capacity to make 125 pieces a day existed before but it was being wasted in the form of unnecessary work and overproduction.

This means that if we regard only work that is needed as real work and define the rest as waste, the following equation holds true whether considering individual workers or the entire line:

$$\text{Present capacity} = \text{work} + \text{waste}$$

True efficiency improvement comes when we produce zero waste and bring the percentage of work to 100 percent. Since, in the Toyota production system, we must make only the amount needed, manpower must be reduced to trim excess capacity and match the needed quantity.

The preliminary step toward application of the Toyota production system is to identify wastes completely:

- Waste of overproduction
- Waste of time on hand (waiting)
- Waste in transportation
- Waste of processing itself

- Waste of stock on hand (inventory)
- Waste of movement
- Waste of making defective products

Eliminating these wastes (see Glossary for categorical explanations) completely can improve the operating efficiency by a large margin. To do this, we must make only the quantity needed, thereby releasing extra manpower. The Toyota production system clearly reveals excess manpower. Because of this, some labor union people have been suspicious of it as a means of laying off workers. But that is not the idea.

Management's responsibility is to identify excess manpower and utilize it effectively. Hiring people when business is good and production is high just to lay them off or recruiting early retirees when recession hits are bad practices. Managers should use them with care. On the other hand, eliminating wasteful and meaningless jobs enhances the value of work for workers.

▸ My Plant-First Principle

The production plant is manufacturing's major source of information. It provides the most direct, current, and stimulating information about management.

I have always firmly believed in the plant-first principle, perhaps because I started out on the plant floor. Even today, as part of top management, I have been unable to separate myself from the reality found in the production plant. The time that provides me with the most vital information about management is the time I spend in the plant, not in the vice president's office.

Some time in 1937-1938, my boss at Toyoda Spinning and Weaving told me to prepare standard work methods for textile work. It was a difficult project. From a book on standard work methods I bought from Maruzen,[1] I managed to do the job.

A proper work procedure, however, cannot be written from a desk. It must be tried and revised many times in the production plant. Furthermore, it must be a procedure that anybody can understand on sight.

When I first came to the Toyota Motor Company during the war, I asked my workers to prepare standard work methods. Skilled workers were being transferred from the production plant to the battlefield and more and more machines were gradually being operated by inexperienced men and women. This naturally increased the need for standard work methods. My experience during that period laid the foundation for my 35 years of work on the Toyota production system. It was also the origin of my plant-first principle.

▶ Writing the Standard Work Sheet Yourself

In each Toyota Motor Company plant, as well as in the production plants of cooperating firms adopting the Toyota production system, visual control is thoroughly established. Standard work sheets are posted prominently at each work station. When one looks up, the *andon* (the line stop indication board) comes into view, showing the location and nature of trouble situations at a glance. Furthermore, boxes containing parts brought to the side of the production line arrive with an attached kanban, the visual symbol of the Toyota production system.

Here, however, I want to discuss the standard work sheet as a means of visual control, which is how the Toyota production system is managed.

Standard work sheets and the information contained in them are important elements of the Toyota production system. For a production person to be able to write a standard work sheet that other workers can understand, he or she must be convinced of its importance.

We have eliminated waste by examining available resources, rearranging machines, improving machining processes, installing autonomous systems, improving tools, analyzing transportation methods, and optimizing the amount of materials at hand for machining. High production efficiency has also been maintained by preventing the recurrence of defective products, operational mistakes, and accidents, and by incorporating workers' ideas. All of this is possible because of the inconspicuous standard work sheet.

The standard work sheet effectively combines materials, workers, and machines to produce efficiently. At Toyota, this procedure is called a work combination. The result is the standard work procedure.

The standard work sheet has changed little since I was first asked to prepare one 40 years ago at the textile plant. However, it is based thoroughly on principles and plays an important role in Toyota's visual control system. It clearly lists the three elements of the standard work procedure as:

1. Cycle time
2. Work sequence
3. Standard inventory

Cycle time is the time allotted to make one piece or unit. This is determined by production quantity; that is, the quantity required and the operating time. Quantity required per day is the quantity required per month divided by that month's number of operating days. Cycle time is computed by dividing operating hours by the quantity required per day. Even when cycle time is determined this way, individual times may differ.

In Japan, it is said that "time is the shadow of motion." In most cases, delay is generated by differences in operator motion and sequence. The job of the field supervisor, section chief, or group foreman is to train workers. I have always said that it should take only three days to train new workers in proper work procedures. When instruction in the sequence and key motions is clear, workers quickly learn to avoid redoing a job or producing defective parts.

To do this, however, the trainer must actually take the hands of the workers and teach them. This generates trust in the supervisor. At the same time, workers must be taught to help each other. Because people are doing the work, rather than machines, there will be individual differences in work times caused by physical conditions. These differences will be absorbed by the first worker in the process, just as in the baton touch zone in track relay. Carrying out the standard work methods in the cycle time helps worker harmony grow.

The term "work sequence" means just what it says. It does not refer to the order of processes along which products flow. It refers rather to the sequence of operations, or the order of operations in which a worker processes items: transporting them, mounting them on machines, removing them from machines, and so on.

Standard inventory refers to the minimum intra-process work-in-process needed for operations to proceed. This includes items mounted on machines.

Even without changing machine layout, standard inventory between processes is generally unnecessary if work is carried out in the order of machining processes. All that is needed are the items mounted on the various machines. On the other hand, one item's worth (or two where two items are mounted on machines) of standard inventory will be required if work proceeds by machine function rather than by the process flow.

In the Toyota production system, the fact that parts have to arrive just-in-time means that standard inventories have to be met that much more rigorously.

▸ Teamwork Is Everything

I touched on the subject of harmony in discussing cycle times. Now I would like to spend some time giving you my thoughts on teamwork.

Work and sports have many things in common. In Japan, competition is traditionally individual, as in *sumo* wrestling, *kendō* swordsmanship, and *judo*. In fact, in Japan we do not "compete" in these activities but rather we "seek the way and study it" devotedly. This approach has its analogy in the work arena, where the art of the individual craftsman is highly valued.

Competitive team sports came to Japan after Western culture was imported. And in modern industry, harmony among people in a group, as in teamwork, is in greater demand than the art of the individual craftsman.

For example, in a boat race with eight rowers per boat, a baseball team with nine players, a volleyball game with six people per side, or a soccer team with eleven members, the key to winning or losing is teamwork. Even with one or two star players, a team does not necessarily win.

Manufacturing is also done through teamwork. It might take 10 or 15 workers, for example, to take a job from raw materials to finished product. The idea is teamwork — not how many parts were machined or drilled by one worker, but how many products were completed by the line as a whole.

Years ago, I used to tell production workers one of my favorite stories about a boat rowed by eight men, four on the left side and four on the right side. If they do not row correctly, the boat will zigzag erratically.

One rower might feel he is stronger than the next and row twice as hard. But this extra effort upsets the boat's progress and moves it off course. The best way to propel the boat faster is for everyone to distribute force equally, rowing evenly and at the same depth.

Today a volleyball team has six players; previously there were nine. If a nine-member team tried to play a six-member team using the same plays, players might be injured bumping into one another. They would probably lose also because having more players is not necessarily an advantage.

Teamwork combined with other factors can allow a smaller team to win. The same is true in a work environment.

Sports gives us so many helpful hints. In baseball, for example, if someone drew boundaries around the infield defense zone and said only the second baseman could play there while the third baseman could only play in another designated area, the game would not be as much fun to watch.

Similarly, at work things do not necessarily run smoothly just because areas of responsibility have been assigned. Teamwork is essential.

► The Skill of Passing the Baton

About the time I began work on the Toyota production system, the Korean War was coming to an end. Newspapers were calling the so-called 38th parallel a national tragedy. The same is true in work. We cannot draw a "38th parallel" in each other's work area.

The work arena is like a track relay — there is always an area where the baton may be passed. If the baton is passed well, the total final time can be better than the individual times of the four runners. In a swimming relay, a swimmer cannot dive before the previous swimmer's hand touches the wall. In track, however, rules are different and a strong runner can make up for a weak runner. This is an interesting point.

In a manufacturing job done by four or five people, the parts should be handed over as if they were batons. If an operator in a later process is delayed, others should help set up his or her machine. When the work area returns to normal, that worker should get the baton and everyone else should return to their positions. I always tell workers they should be skillful in baton passing.

In work and in sports, it is desirable for team members to work with equal strength. In actuality, this is not always the case, particularly with new employees who are unfamiliar with the work. At Toyota, we call the baton-passing system the "Mutual Assistance Campaign." It provides the power to generate more powerful teamwork.

I feel the most important point in common between sports and work is the continuing need for practice and training. It is easy to understand theory with the mind; the problem is to remember it with the body. The goal is to know and do instinctively. Having the spirit to endure the training is the first step on the road to winning.

► An Idea from the U.S. Supermarket

To repeat, the two pillars of the Toyota production system are just-in-time and automation with a human touch, or autonomation. The tool used to operate the system is kanban, an idea I got from American supermarkets.

Following World War II, American products flowed into Japan — chewing gum and Coca-Cola, even the jeep. The first U.S.-style supermarket appeared in the mid-1950s. And, as more and more Japanese people visited the United States, they saw the intimate relationship between the supermarket and the style of daily life in America. Consequently, this type of store became the rage in Japan due to Japanese curiosity and fondness for imitation.

In 1956, I toured U.S. production plants at General Motors, Ford, and other machinery companies. But my strongest impression was the extent of the supermarket's prevalence in America. The reason for this was that by the late 1940s, at Toyota's machine shop that I managed, we were already studying the U.S. supermarket and applying its methods to our work.

Combining automobiles and supermarkets may seem odd. But for a long time, since learning about the setup of supermarkets in America, we made a connection between supermarkets and the just-in-time system.

A supermarket is where a customer can get (1) what is needed, (2) at the time needed, (3) in the amount needed. Sometimes, of course, a customer may buy more than he or she needs. In principle, however, the supermarket is a place where we buy according to need. Supermarket operators, therefore, must make certain that customers can buy what they need at any time.

Compared to Japan's traditional, turn-of-the-century merchandising methods such as peddling medicines door to door, going around to customers to take orders, and hawking wares, America's supermarket system is more rational. From the seller's viewpoint, labor is not wasted carrying items that may not sell, while the buyer does not have to worry about whether to buy extra items.

From the supermarket we got the idea of viewing the earlier process in a production line as a kind of store. The later process (customer) goes to the earlier process (supermarket) to acquire the required parts (commodities) at the time and in the quantity needed. The earlier process immediately produces the quantity just taken (restocking the shelves). We hoped that this would help us approach our just-in-time goal and, in

1953, we actually applied the system in our machine shop at the main plant.

In the 1950s, American-style supermarkets appeared in Japan, bringing the object of our research even closer. And when in America in 1956, I finally fulfilled my desire to visit a supermarket firsthand.

Our biggest problem with this system was how to avoid throwing the earlier process into confusion when a later process picked up large quantities at a time. Eventually, after trial and error, we came up with production leveling, described later in the book.

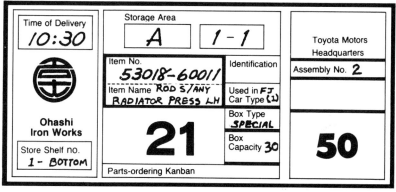

When the Ohashi Iron Works delivers parts to the headquarters factory of Toyota Motors, they use this parts-ordering kanban for subcontractors. The number 50 represents the number of Toyota's receiving gate. The rod is delivered to storage area A. The number 21 is an item back number for the parts.

Figure 1. A Sample of Kanban

► What Is Kanban?

The operating method of the Toyota production system is *kanban*. Its most frequently used form is a piece of paper contained in a rectangular vinyl envelope.

This piece of paper carries information that can be divided into three categories: (1) pickup information, (2) transfer information, and (3) production information. The kanban carries the information vertically and laterally within Toyota itself and between Toyota and the cooperating firms.

As I said earlier, the idea came from the supermarket. Suppose we take kanban into the supermarket. How would it work?

Commodities purchased by customers are checked out through the cash register. Cards that carry information about the types and quantities of commodities bought are then forwarded to the purchasing department. Using this information, commodities taken are swiftly replaced by purchasing. These cards correspond to the withdrawal kanban in the Toyota production system. In the supermarket, the commodities displayed in the store correspond to the inventory at the production plant.

If a supermarket had its own production plant nearby, there would be production kanban in addition to the withdrawal kanban between the store and the production department. From the directions on this kanban, the production department would produce the number of commodities picked up.

Of course, supermarkets have not gone that far. In our production plant, however, we have been doing this from the beginning.

The supermarket system was adopted in the machine shop around 1953. To make it work, we used pieces of paper listing the part number of a piece and other information related to machining work. We called this "kanban."

Subsequently, this was called the "kanban system." We felt that if this system were used skillfully, all movements in the plant could be unified or systematized. After all, one piece of paper provided at a glance the following information: production quantity, time, method, sequence or transfer quantity, transfer time, destination, storage point, transfer equipment, container, and so on. At the time, I did not doubt that this means of conveying information would certainly work.

Generally in a business, *what*, *when*, and *how many* are generated by the work planning section in the form of a work start plan, transfer plan, production order, or delivery order passed through the plant. When this system is used, "when" is set arbitrarily and people think it will be all right whether parts arrive on time or early. Managing parts made too early, however, means carrying a lot of intermediate workers. The word "just" in "just-in-time" means exactly that. If parts arrive anytime prior to their need — not at the precise time needed — waste cannot be eliminated.

In the Toyota production system, overproduction is completely prevented by kanban. As a result, there is no need for extra inventory and, consequently, there is no need for the warehouse and its manager. Generation of countless paper slips also becomes unnecessary.

► Incorrect Use Causes Problems

With a better tool, we can get wonderful results. But if we use it incorrectly, the tool can make things worse.

Kanban is one of those tools that if used improperly can cause a variety of problems. To employ kanban properly and skillfully, we tried to clearly understand its purpose and role and then establish rules for its use.

Kanban is a way to achieve just-in-time; its purpose is just-in-time. Kanban, in essence, becomes the autonomic nerve of the production line. Based on this, production workers start work by themselves, and make their own decisions concerning overtime. The kanban system also makes clear what must be done by managers and supervisors. This unquestionably promotes improvement in both work and equipment.

The goal of eliminating waste is also highlighted by kanban. Its use immediately shows what is waste, allowing for creative study and improvement proposals. In the production plant, kanban is a powerful force to reduce manpower and inventory, eliminate defective products, and prevent the recurrence of breakdowns.

It is not an overstatement to say that kanban controls the flow of goods at Toyota. It controls the production of a company exceeding $4.8 billion a year.

In this way, Toyota's kanban system clearly reflects our wishes. It is practiced under strict rules and its effectiveness is shown by our company's achievements. The Toyota production system, however, advances by the minute and close supervision of the kanban rules is a neverending problem.

Functions of kanban	Rules for use
1. Provides pick-up or transport information.	1. Later process picks up the number of items indicated by the kanban at the earlier process.
2. Provides production information.	2. Earlier process produces items in the quantity and sequence indicated by the kanban.
3. Prevents overproduction and excessive transport.	3. No items are made or transported without a kanban.
4. Serves as a work order attached to goods.	4. Always attach a kanban to the goods.
5. Prevents defective products by identifying the process making the defectives.	5. Defective products are not sent on to the subsequent process. The result is 100% defect-free goods.
6. Reveals existing problems and maintains inventory control.	6. Reducing the number of kanban increases their sensitivity.

▸ The Talent and Courage to Rethink What We Call Common Sense

The first rule of kanban is that the later process goes to the earlier process to pick up products. This rule was derived from need and from looking at things upside-down, or from the opposite standpoint.

To practice this first rule, a superficial understanding is not enough. Top management must change its way of thinking and make a commitment to reverse the conventional flow of production, transfer, and delivery. This will meet with lots of resistance and requires courage. The greater the commitment, however, the more successful will be the implementation of the Toyota production system.

In the 30 years since I moved from textiles to the world of automobiles, I have worked continuously to develop and promote the Toyota production system, even though I doubted my ability to succeed.

This may sound presumptuous, but the growth of the Toyota production system has tended to coincide with the growth of my own responsibilities at Toyota.

In 1949-1950, as manager of the machine shop in what is now the main plant, I made the first step toward the "just-in-time" idea. Then, to establish the flow of production, we rearranged the machines and adopted a multi-process system that assigns one operator to three or four machines. From then on, I utilized my growing authority to its fullest extent to expand these ideas.

During this period, all the ideas I boldly put into practice were intended to improve the old, conservative production system — and they might have looked high-handed. Toyota's top management watched the situation quietly, and I admire the attitude they took.

I have a good reason for emphasizing the role of top management in discussing the first rule of kanban. There are many obstacles to implementing the rule that the later process must take what it requires from the earlier process when it is needed. For this reason, management commitment and strong support are essential to the successful application of this first rule.

To the earlier process, however, this means eliminating the production schedule they have relied upon for so long. Production workers have a good deal of psychological resistance to the idea that simply producing as much as possible is no longer a priority.

Trying to make only the items withdrawn also means changing the setup more often unless the production line is dedicated to one item. Usually, people consider it an advantage for the earlier process to make a large quantity of one item. But while producing item A in quantity, the process may not meet the need for item B. Consequently, shortening setup time and reducing lot sizes becomes necessary.

Among the new problems, the most difficult surface when the later process picks up a large quantity of one item. When this happens, the earlier process immediately runs out of that item. If we try to counter this by holding some inventory, however, we will not know which item will be withdrawn next and will have to keep an inventory of each item: A, B, and so on. If all earlier processes start doing this, piles of inventory will form in every corner of the plant.

Therefore, to realize a system in which the later process picks up requires us to transform the production methods of both the earlier and the later processes.

Step by step, I solved the problems related to the system of withdrawal by the later process. There was no manual and we could find out what would happen only by trying. Tension increased daily as we tried and corrected and then tried and corrected again. Repeating this, I expanded the system of pickup by the later process within the company. Experiments were always carried out at a plant within the company that did not deal with parts ordered from outside. The idea was to exhaust the new system's problems within the company first.

In 1963, we started handling the delivery of the parts ordered from outside. It took nearly 20 years. Today we frequently hear a chassis maker asking the cooperating firm to bring parts just-in-time as if "just-in-time" was the most convenient system. However, if used for picking up parts ordered from outside without first changing the production method within the company, kanban immediately becomes a dangerous weapon.

Just-in-time is an ideal system in which the items needed arrive at the side of the production line at the time and in the quantity needed. But a chassis maker cannot simply ask the cooperating firm to employ this system, because adopting just-in-time means completely overhauling the existing production system. Therefore, once decided upon, it should be undertaken with a firm and determined mind.

► Establishing the Flow Is the Basic Condition

After World War II, our main concern was how to produce high quality goods and we helped the cooperating firms in this area. After 1955, however, the question became how to make the exact quantity needed. Then, after the oil crisis, we started teaching outside firms how to produce goods using the kanban system.

Prior to that, the Toyota Group guided cooperating firms on work or production methods, in the Toyota system. Outsiders seem to think that the Toyota system and kanban are the same thing. But the Toyota production system is the production method and the kanban system is the way it is managed.

So, up until the oil crisis, we were teaching Toyota's production methods, focusing on how to make goods as much as possible in a continuous flow. With this groundwork already done, it was very easy to give guidance to Toyota's cooperating firms on kanban.

Unless one completely grasps this method of doing work so that things will flow, it is impossible to go right into the kanban system when the time comes. The Toyota Group was able to adopt and somehow digest it because the production plant already understood and practiced the idea of establishing a flow. When people have no concept of this, it is very difficult to introduce the kanban system.

When we first tried to use the kanban system on the final assembly line, going to a machine shop of an earlier process to withdraw the items needed at the time and in the quantity needed never worked. This was only natural and not the fault of the machine shop. We realized that the system would not work unless we set up a production flow that could handle the kanban system going back process by process.

Kanban is a tool for realizing just–in–time. For this tool to work fairly well, the production processes must be managed to flow as much as possible. This is really the basic condition. Other important conditions are leveling production as much as possible and always working in accordance with standard work methods.

At Toyota's main plant, the flow between the final assembly line and the machining line was established in 1950 and the synchronization started on a small scale. From there, we kept going in reverse toward the earlier processes. We gradually laid the groundwork for the company-wide adoption of kanban so that the work and transferring of parts could be done under the kanban system. This happened gradually by gaining the understanding of all people involved.

It was only in 1962 that we could manage the kanban system company-wide. After achieving this, we called the cooperating firms and asked them to study it by watching how it really worked. These people knew nothing about kanban and making them understand it without a textbook was difficult.

We asked the cooperating firms from nearby to come, a few at a time, to study the system. For example, the outside die press people came to see our die press operation and the machine shop people came to see our machine shop. This way of teaching gave us the ability to demonstrate an efficient production method in an actual production plant. As a matter of fact, they would have had difficulty understanding the system without seeing it in action.

This teaching effort started with the cooperating firms nearby and spread to the Nagoya district. In the outlying Kanto district, however, progress was delayed in part due to the distance. However, a bigger reason was because part makers in the Kanto district were supplying their products not only to Toyota but to other companies as well. They felt they could not use the kanban system just with Toyota.[2]

We decided that this would take time for them to understand, and we set out patiently. In the beginning, the cooperating firms saw kanban as troublesome. Of course, no top management came; no directors in charge of production or managers of production departments showed up in the beginning. Usually people in charge of the operation would come, but no one very important.

At first, I believe, many firms came without knowing what was involved. But we wanted them to understand kanban and if they didn't, Toyota employees would go and help. People from nearby firms understood the system early although they faced resistance in their companies. And today it is a pleasure to see all this effort bear fruit.

▶ Use Your Authority to Encourage Them

In the beginning, everyone resisted kanban because it seemed to contradict conventional wisdom. Therefore, I had to experiment with kanban within my own sphere of authority. Of course, we tried to avoid interfering with the regular work going on.

In the 1940s, I was in charge of the machine shop and the assembly line. At the time, there was only one plant. By the end of the labor dispute in 1950, there were two production departments in the main plant, No. 1 and No. 2. I managed the latter. Kanban could not be tried in No. 1 because its forging and casting processes would affect the plant as a whole. Kanban could be applied only in No. 2's machining and assembly processes.

I soon became manager of the Motomachi plant when it was completed in 1959 and began experimenting with kanban there. Because the crude materials came from the main plant, however, kanban could be used only between the machine shop, press shop, and assembly line.

In 1962, I was named manager of the main plant. Only then was kanban implemented in forging and casting, making it a company-wide system at last.

It took 10 years to establish kanban at the Toyota Motor Company. Although it sounds like a long time, I think it was natural because we were breaking in totally new concepts. It was, nonetheless, a valuable experience.

To make kanban understood throughout the company, we had to involve everyone. If the manager of the production department understood it while the workers did not, kanban would not have worked. At the foreman level, people seemed quite lost because they were learning something totally different from conventional practice.

I could yell at a foreman under my jurisdiction, but not at a foreman from the neighboring department. Thus, getting people in every corner of the plant to understand naturally took a long time.

During this period, Toyota's top manager was a man of great vision who, without a word, left the operation entirely to me. When I was — rather forcefully — urging foremen in the production plant to understand kanban, my boss received a considerable number of complaints. They voiced the feeling that this fellow Ohno was doing something utterly ridiculous and should be stopped. This must have put the top manager in a difficult position at times, but even then he must have trusted me. I was not told to stop and for this I am grateful.

In 1962, kanban was adopted company-wide; it had earned its recognition. After that, we entered a high-growth period — the timing was excellent. I think the gradual spread of kanban made possible the strong production yield.

While in charge of the assembly line, I applied the just-in-time system there. The most important processes for assembly were the earlier processes of machining and body painting. The bodies came from the die press section. The machining process was difficult to connect by kanban to the crude material section but we were satisfied to accumulate experience as we worked to link up the machining process. This period was valuable because we could identify kanban's inadequacies.

▸ Mountains Should Be Low and
   Valleys Should Be Shallow

To make the second rule of kanban work (having the earlier process produce only the amount withdrawn by the later process) manpower and equipment in each production process must be prepared in every respect to produce the quantities needed at the time needed.

In this case, if the later process withdraws unevenly in terms of time and quantity, the earlier process must have extra manpower and equipment to accommodate its requests. This becomes a heavy burden. The greater the fluctuation in quantity picked up, the more excess capacity is required by the earlier process.

To make matters worse, the Toyota production system is tied through synchronization not only to each production process within the Toyota Motor Company but also to the production processes of the cooperating firms outside Toyota using kanban. Because of this, fluctuations in production and orders at Toyota's final process have a negative impact on all earlier processes.

To avoid the occurrence of such negative cycles, the large chassis maker, specifically Toyota's final automobile assembly line (the "first process"), must lower the peaks and raise the valleys in production as much as possible so that the flow surface is smooth. This is called production leveling, or load smoothing, in the Toyota production system.

Ideally, leveling should result in zero fluctuation at the final assembly line, or the last process. This is very difficult, however, because more than 200,000 cars monthly come off the several assembly lines at Toyota in an almost infinite number of varieties.

The number of varieties reaches thousands just by considering the combinations of car size and style, body type, engine size, and transmission method. If we include colors and combinations of various options, we will rarely see completely identical cars.

Modern society's diverse wants and values are clearly seen in the variety of cars. In fact, it is certainly this diversity that has reduced the effectiveness of mass production in the automobile industry. In adapting to this diversity, the Toyota production system has been much more efficient than the Ford-style mass-production system developed in America.

Toyota's production system was originally conceived to produce small quantities of many types for the Japanese environment. Consequently, on this foundation it evolved into a production system that can meet the challenge of diversification.

While the traditional planned mass-production system does not respond easily to change, the Toyota production system is very elastic and can take the difficult conditions imposed by diverse market demands and digest them. The Toyota system has the flexibility to do this.

After the oil crisis, people started paying attention to the Toyota production system. I would like to make clear that the reasons lie in the system's unsurpassed flexibility in adapting to changing conditions. This capacity is the source of its strength even in a low-growth period when quantity does not increase.

▸ Challenge to Production Leveling

Let me tell a story about a specific case of production leveling. In Toyota's Tsutsumi plant, production is leveled on two assembly lines making passenger cars: Corona, Carina, and Celica.

In one line, the Corona and Carina flow alternately. They do not run Coronas in the morning and Carinas in the afternoon. This is to maintain a level load. The lot size for single items is kept as small as possible. Great care is taken to avoid generating undesirable fluctuation in the earlier process.

Even the production of large numbers of Coronas is leveled. For example, suppose we make 10,000 Coronas working 20 days a month. Assume that this breaks down to 5,000 sedans, 2,500 hardtops, and 2,500 wagons. This means that 250 sedans, 125 hardtops, and 125 wagons are made daily. These are arranged on the production line as follows: one sedan, one hardtop, then a sedan, then a wagon, and so on. This way, the lot size and fluctuation in production can be minimized.

The finely tuned production carried out in the final automobile assembly line is Toyota's mass production process. That this type of production can be carried out demonstrates that the earlier processes, such as the die press section, have settled into the new system after breaking away from the traditional planned mass-production system.

In the beginning, the idea of leveling to reduce lot size and minimize the mass production of single items placed too heavy a demand on the die press section. It had been a long-accepted production fact that continuous punching with one die in the press brings the cost down. It was considered common sense to produce in the largest lots possible and punch continuously without stopping the press.

The Toyota production system, however, requires leveled production and the smallest lots possible even though it seems contrary to conventional wisdom. So, how did the die press section cope with this problem?

Making lots small means we cannot punch with one die for very long. To respond to the dizzying variety in product types, the die must be changed often. Consequently, setup procedures must be done quickly.

The same is true for other machine sections, all the way back to the earlier processes. Even the cooperating firms supplying parts are using buzz words like "reduce lot size" and "shorten setup time" — ideas completely contrary to past practice.

In the 1940s, Toyota's die changes took two to three hours. As production leveling spread through the company in the 1950s, setup times went to less than one hour and as little as 15 minutes. By the late 1960s, it was down to a mere 3 minutes.

In summary, the need for quick die changes was generated and steps were taken to eliminate the adjustments — something never discussed in previous work manuals. To do this, everybody chipped in with ideas while workers were trained to shorten changeover times. Within the Toyota Motor Company and its cooperating firms, people's desire to achieve the new system intensified beyond description. The system became the product of their effort.

► Production Leveling and Market Diversification

As I already mentioned, production leveling is much more advantageous than the planned mass-production system in responding to the diverse demands of the automobile market.

We can say this with confidence. Generally speaking, however, diversification of the market and production leveling will not necessarily be in harmony from the beginning. They have aspects that do not accommodate each other.

It is undeniable that leveling becomes more difficult as diversification develops. However, I want to emphasize again that, with effort, the Toyota production system can cope with it well enough. In keeping market diversification and production leveling in harmony, it is important to avoid the use of dedicated facilities and equipment that could have more general utility.

For example, taking the Corolla, the world's largest mass-produced car in 1978, a definite production plan can be set up on a monthly basis. The total cars needed can be divided by the number of work days (the number of days on which actual production can be carried out) to level the number of cars to be made per day.

On the production line, even finer leveling must be done. To let sedans or coupes flow continuously during a fixed time interval is contrary to leveling in that the same item is allowed to flow in a batch. Of course, if two production lines were used, one for sedans and one for coupes exclusively, leveling would be easier.

But this is not possible because of restrictions in space and equipment. What can be done? If one production line is set up so that sedans and coupes can both be assembled in any sequence, then leveling would be possible.

Viewed from this perspective, mass production using dedicated facilities, once the strongest weapon for reducing cost, is not necessarily the best choice. Of increasing importance are efforts to put together specialized, yet versatile production processes through the use of machines and jigs that can handle minimal quantities of materials. More effort is needed to find the minimum facilities and equipment required for general use. To do this, we must utilize all available knowledge to avoid undermining the benefits of mass production.

By studying every process like this, we can keep diversification and production leveling in harmony and still respond to customer orders in a timely manner. As market demands grow more diverse, we must put even more emphasis on this point.

▸ Kanban Accelerates Improvements

Under its first and second rules, kanban serves as a withdrawal order, an order for conveyance or delivery, and as a work order. Rule three of kanban prohibits picking up or producing goods without a kanban. Rule four requires a kanban to be attached to the goods. Rule five requires 100 percent defect-free products (that is, do not send anything defective to the subsequent process). Rule six urges us to reduce the number of kanban. When these rules are faithfully practiced, the role of kanban expands.

A kanban always moves with the needed goods and so becomes a work order for each process. In this way, a kanban can prevent overproduction, the largest loss in production.

To ensure that we have 100 percent defect-free products, we must set up a system that automatically informs us if any process generates defective products; that is, a system in which the process generating defective products feels the pinch. This is indeed where the kanban system is unrivaled.

Processes producing in a just-in-time system do not need extra inventory. So, if the prior process generates defective parts, the next process must stop the line. Furthermore, everyone sees when this happens and the defective part is returned to the earlier process. It is an embarrassing situation meant to help prevent the recurrence of such defects.

If the meaning of "defective" goes beyond defective parts to include defective work, then the meaning of "100 percent defect-free products" becomes clearer. In other words, insufficient standardization and rationalization[3] creates waste (*muda*), inconsistency (*mura*), and unreasonableness (*muri*) in work procedures and work hours that eventually lead to the production of defective products.

Unless such defective work is reduced, it is difficult to assure an adequate supply for the later process to withdraw or to achieve the objective of producing as cheaply as possible. Efforts to thoroughly stabilize and rationalize the processes are the key to successful implementation of automation. Only with this foundation can production leveling be effective.

It takes a great effort to practice the six rules of kanban discussed above. In reality, practicing these rules means nothing less than adopting the Toyota production system as the management system of the whole company.

Introducing kanban without actually practicing these rules will bring neither the control expected of kanban nor the cost reduction. Thus, a half-hearted introduction of kanban brings a hundred harms and not a single gain. Anyone who recognizes the effectiveness of kanban as a production management tool for reducing cost must be determined to observe the rules and overcome all obstacles.

It is said that improvement is eternal and infinite. It should be the duty of those working with kanban to keep improving it with creativity and resourcefulness without allowing it to become fixed at any stage.

▸ Carrying Carts as Kanban

I have described the kanban as the piece of paper contained in a rectangular vinyl envelope. An important role of kanban is to provide the information that connects the earlier and later processes at every level.

A kanban always accompanies the goods and thus is the essential communications tool for just-in-time production. In the following case, the kanban functions even more effectively when combined with carrying carts.

In Toyota's main plant, a carrying cart of limited load capacity is used to pick up the assembled engines and transmissions in the final assembly line. A kanban is attached to the engine, for example, carried on this carrying cart.

But the carrying cart itself simultaneously performs the role of a kanban. Thus, when the standard number of engines at the side of the final assembly line (three to five units) is reached, the worker in the section that attaches the engine to the vehicle takes the vacant carrying cart to the engine assembly point (the earlier process), picks up a cart loaded with the necessary engines, and leaves the vacant carrying cart.

In principle, a kanban should be attached. In this case, however, even if the kanban itself is not attached to the carrying cart, the earlier and later processes can talk to each other, decide on the number of carrying carts to be used, and agree on the pickup rules so that the same effectiveness can be achieved by using simple number plates.

For example, when there is no vacant cart in the unit assembly line, there is no place to put completed units. Overproduction is automatically checked even if someone wants to make more. The final assembly line also cannot hold any extra inventory other than that on the carrying carts.

As the basic idea of kanban spreads throughout manufacturing, many tools like the carrying cart kanban can be devised. Nonetheless, we should not forget to always use the principles of kanban.

Let me raise another example. In an automobile production plant, chain conveyers are used as a way to rationalize, or improve, transportation. Parts can be suspended from the conveyor while being painted or carried to the assembly line on it. Of course, it goes without saying that no part can be hung on the conveyor without a kanban on the hanger.

When many types of parts are carried by this chain conveyer, indicators designating the parts needed are attached to the hangers at regular intervals to eliminate any mistake in the type of part, quantity, or time it is required. Thus, by installing a means of conveying only the parts indicated, smooth delivery and withdrawal of needed parts can be achieved. Production leveling is maintained by circulating the part-indicators with the conveyer.

► The Elastic Nature of Kanban

I would like to give another example that demonstrates the true meaning of kanban.

The propeller shaft is an important auto part that causes problems sporadically in assembly. To prevent uneven rotation, workers attach small pieces of iron as balance weights during the finishing stage.

There are five types of balance weights. A piece suitable for a particular degree of imbalance in the propeller shaft is selected from the five types and attached. If there is no imbalance, no balance weight is needed.

In some cases, many pieces have to be attached. The number of different balance weights used is irregular. Unlike ordinary parts, the amount needed is not known when the production plan is written. Thus, with these parts, unless production is well managed, an urgent need may arise, while in other cases, unnecessary inventory piles up.

We might say this is not a serious problem because it is only a small piece of iron. In reality, however, it is a big problem because extra indirect workers may be kept idle. This is yet another challenge to Toyota's kanban system.

Kanban must work effectively to maintain just-in-time in the plant. And for kanban to be effective, stabilization and production leveling are indispensable conditions. Some people think, however, that kanban can be used only to manage parts processed in daily stable quantities — but this is a mistake. Others think kanban cannot be used without a steady withdrawal of parts. This is also wrong thinking.

Kanban was introduced to manage the balance weight problem, one of the most difficult processes in automobile production. Since the amount was not stable, the first step toward effectively managing the production, transfer, and use of the balance weight was to know at all times how many of the five weights were held in each process. With these amounts in mind, we had to find a way to trigger production or transfer so that an urgent need or excess inventory could not arise.

What was the result? By attaching a kanban to the actual balance weights, types and quantities available could be identified accurately. With the kanban circulating between the processes, production and transfer of the parts could be initiated in the necessary sequence at all times. As a result, inventories of the five weights were kept constant and, eventually, reduced drastically.

The kanban system is not inflexible or stiff. As Toyota's experience with the balance weights demonstrates, kanban is an effective tool even for management of special parts where the amount used is unstable and where kanban may seem inapplicable at first.

3
▼

Further Development

An Autonomic Nervous System in the
Business Organization

A BUSINESS ORGANIZATION is like the human body. The human body contains autonomic nerves that work without regard to human wishes and motor nerves that react to human command to control muscles. The human body has an amazing structure and operation; the fine balance and precision with which body parts are accommodated in the overall design are even more marvelous.

In the human body, the autonomic nerve causes us to salivate when we see tasty food. It accelerates our heart rate during exercise so that circulation is enhanced. It performs other similar functions that respond automatically to changes in the body. These functions are performed unconsciously without any directive from the brain.

At Toyota, we began to think about how to install an autonomic nervous system in our own rapidly growing business organization. In our production plant, an autonomic nerve means making judgments autonomously at the lowest possible level; for example, when to stop production, what sequence to follow in making parts, or when overtime is necessary to produce the required amount.

These discussions can be made by factory workers themselves, without having to consult the production control or engineering departments that correspond to the brain in the human body. The plant should be a place where such judgments can be made by workers autonomously.

In Toyota's case, I believe this autonomic nervous system grew as the idea of just-in-time penetrated broadly and deeply into the production field, and as adherence to the rules increased through the use of kanban. As I thought about the business organization and the autonomic nerves in the human body, the concepts began to interconnect, overlap, and stir my imagination.

In actual business practice, the production control department, as the center of operation, sends out various directives. These plans must then be altered continuously. Because these plans are what really affect a business's present and future, we could say they correspond to the backbone in the human body.

Plans change very easily. Worldly affairs do not always go according to plan and orders have to change rapidly in response to changes in circumstances. If one sticks to the idea that, once set, a plan should not be changed, a business cannot exist for long.

It is said that the sturdier the human spine, the more easily it bends. This elasticity is important. If something goes wrong and the backbone is placed in a cast, this vital area gets stiff and stops functioning. Sticking to a plan once it is set up is like putting the human body in a cast. It is not healthy.

Some people think that acrobats must have soft bones. But this is not true — acrobats are not mollusks. Their strong, flexible backbones enable them to make surprising movements.

The spine of an older person, like myself, does not bend easily. And, once bent, it does not unbend quickly. This is definitely a phenomenon of aging. We observe the same phenomenon in a business.

I think a business should have reflexes that can respond instantly and smoothly to small changes in the plan without having to go to the brain. It is similar to the fluttering reflex action of the eyes when dust is around or the reflex action of a hand pulling away quickly when it touches something hot.

The larger a business, the better reflexes it needs. If a small change in a plan must be accompanied by a brain command to make it work (for example, the production control department issuing order slips and plan change sheets), the business will be unable to avoid burns or injuries and will lose great opportunities.

Building a fine-tuning mechanism into the business so that change will not be felt as change is like implanting a reflex nerve inside the body. Earlier I said visual control is possible through just-in-time and autonomation. I firmly believe that an industrial reflex nerve can be installed by using these two pillars of the Toyota production system.

► Provide Necessary Information When Needed

I have emphasized that an "agricultural" mind at work in the industrial age causes problems. But should we then go to a "computer" mind in one jump? The answer is no. There should be an "industrial" mind between the agricultural and the computer minds.

The computer is indeed a great invention. With computers available, it is a waste to perform calculations by hand. Conventional wisdom dictates that such work be done by computers. In reality, however, the situation seems different. While we intend humans to control them, computers have become so speedy that now it looks as if humans are controlled by the machine.

Is it really economical to provide more information than we need — more quickly than we need it? This is like buying a large, high-performance machine that produces too much. The extra items have to be stored in a warehouse, which raises the cost.

Much of the excess information generated by computers is not needed for production at all. Receiving information too quickly results in early delivery of raw materials, causing waste. Too much information throws the production field into confusion.

The industrial mind extracts knowledge from manufacturing people, gives the knowledge to the machines working as extensions of the workers' hands and feet, and develops the production plan for the entire plant including outside cooperating firms.

America's mass-production system has used computers extensively and effectively. At Toyota, we do not reject the computer, because it is essential in planning production leveling procedures and calculating the number of parts needs daily. We use the computer freely, as a tool, and try not to be pushed around by it. But we reject the dehumanization caused by computers and the way they can lead to higher costs.

Toyota's just-in-time production is a way to deliver exactly what the production line needs when it is needed. This method does not require extra inventory. Similarly, we want information only when we need it. Information sent to production should be timed exactly.

A computer performs instantly calculations that previously took an hour. Its tempo is incompatible with that of people. We can run into completely unexpected situations unless we realize this. Processing customer orders and information on market wants and needs by computer can be very effective. However, information needed for production purposes, although arrived at gradually, is not needed 10 or 20 days in advance.

An industrial mind must be very realistic — and realism is what the Toyota production system is based upon.

▸ The Toyota-Style Information System

Toyota naturally makes production schedules — like other companies. Just because we produce just-in-time in response to market needs, that is, incoming orders from the Toyota Automobile Sales Company, does not mean we can operate without planning. To operate smoothly, Toyota's production schedule and information system must be tightly meshed.

First, the Toyota Motor Company has an annual plan. This means the rough number of cars — for instance, 2 million — to be produced and sold during the current year.

Next, there is the monthly production schedule. For example, the type and quantities of cars to be made in March are announced internally early on, and in February, a more detailed schedule is "set." Both schedules are sent to the outside cooperating firms as they are developed. Based on these plans, the daily production schedule is established in detail and includes production leveling.

In the Toyota production system, the method of setting up this daily schedule is important. During the last half of the previous month, each production line is informed of the daily production quantity for each product type. At Toyota, this is called the daily level. On the other hand, the daily sequence schedule is sent only to one place — the final assembly line. This is a special characteristic of Toyota's information system. In other companies, scheduling information is sent to every production process.

This is how the Toyota information system works in production: when the production line workers use parts at the side of the line for assembly, they remove the kanban. The preceding process makes as many parts as were used, eliminating the need for a special production schedule. In other words, the kanban acts as a production order for the earlier processes.

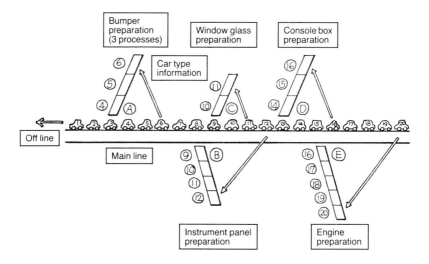

Figure 2. Automobile Assembly Line

For example, Figure #2 depicts the final body assembly line in an automobile plant. Each sub-assembly process combines with the main line in the middle to form the production line. The numbers in the illustration are the car pass numbers. Thus, Car #1 is about to come off the line and Car #20 has just entered Process #1.

The production order, or sequence schedule, is issued to Process #1 for each car (in this example, specifications for Car #20 are issued). The worker at Process #1 attaches a sheet of paper (production order sheet) to this car with all the information needed for its production (that is, the information indicating what kind of car it is). The workers in processes following Process #2 can tell which parts to use for assembly by looking at the car.

Workers in the sub-processes can also tell what to do as soon as they can see the car. If the car is not visible because it is blocked by equipment or pillars, information is passed by kanban in the following way:

Suppose bumpers are being assembled on the main line in Process A. Let's call the process where bumpers are prepared Subprocess 3. Process A needs to know what type of bumper goes on Car 6. Therefore, the process on the main assembly line assembling Car 6 gives the information to Process A on a kanban. No other information is needed.

Computers could relay such information to each process when it is needed. Setting up the computers, however, requires equipment and wiring that are not only expensive but often unreliable. With the computers of today, Car #20's information is issued to Process A and to the main line at the same time. But, at that moment, Process A needs information only on Car #6 — not on Car #20.

Too much information induces us to produce ahead and can also cause a mix-up in sequence. Items might not be produced when needed, or too many might be made, some with defects. Eventually, it becomes impossible to make a simple change in the production schedule.

In business, excess information must be suppressed. Toyota suppresses it by letting the products being produced carry the information.

► Fine Adjustment

Automatic adjustments are an important effect in production if we organize the information system as just described.

With market predictions and the automobile in general, quantities and product types shift constantly with or without a big economic crisis. To cope with a constantly fluctuating market, the production line must be able to respond to schedule changes. In reality, however, the information system and production constraints make change difficult.

An important characteristic of kanban is that within certain limits it makes fine adjustments automatically. A line does not have detailed schedules beforehand and so does not know what type of car to assemble until the kanban is removed and read. For example, it anticipates four Car A's and six Car B's for a total of 10 cars. But in the end, the ratio might turn out to be the reverse — six Car A's and four Car B's.

Reversed ratios, however, do not cause someone to run around announcing the change. It happens simply because the production process follows the information carried by the kanban. Kanban's value is that it allows this degree of change to be handled automatically. If we ignore market fluctuations and fail to make adjustments accordingly, sooner or later we will have to make a big change in scheduling.

For example, by sticking to a production schedule for three months despite a 5 to 10 percent sales slump, we might be forced to cut production by 30 to 40 percent in one jump four or five months later under the guise of inventory adjustment. This would cause problems not only within the company but in the cooperating firms as well. The larger the business, the greater the social impact — and this could be a serious problem.

Sticking to a schedule once it is established, regardless of circumstances, is how things are done under a controlled (or planned) economy. I don't believe the fine adjustments in production made possible by using kanban will work in controlled economies where initial production plans never vary.

▸ Coping with Changes

The term "fine adjustment" has a hidden meaning that should be understood, especially by top management. Everyone knows that things do not always go according to plan. But there are people in the world who recklessly try to force a schedule even though they know it may be impossible. They will say "It's good to follow the schedule" or "It's a shame to change the plan," and will do anything to make it work. But as long as we cannot accurately predict the future, our actions should change to suit changing situations. In industry, it is important to enable production people to cope with change and think flexibly.

I myself have struggled for a long time with a production system not easily understood by others. Looking back at the route I have persistently taken, I believe I can safely recommend: "Correct a mistake immediately — to rush and not take time to correct a problem causes work loss later." I also say, "Wait for the right opportunity." These ideas developed from kanban, the tool that kept us from failure and misjudgment.

I believe the role of fine adjustments is not only to indicate whether a schedule change is a "go" or a "temporary stop," but also to enable us to find out why a stop occurred and how to make the fine adjustments necessary to make it go again. The Toyota production system is still not perfect. More development is needed on fine adjustments.

I naturally prefer a free economy over a controlled one. Today, however, the value of private enterprise is frequently questioned and it is imperative that everyone be qualified and flexible enough to make fine adjustments when they are needed.

▸ What Is True Economy?

"Economy" is a word used daily but rarely understood, even in business. Particularly in business, the pursuit of true economy is tied directly to its survival. Therefore, we must consider this point seriously.

In the Toyota production system, we think of economy in terms of manpower reduction and cost reduction. The relationship between these two elements is clearer if we consider a manpower reduction policy as a means of realizing cost reduction, the most critical condition for a business's survival and growth.

Manpower reduction at Toyota is a company-wide activity whose purpose is cost reduction. Therefore, all considerations and improvement ideas, when boiled down, must be tied to cost reduction. Saying this in reverse, the criterion of all decisions is whether cost reduction can be achieved.

Two other issues in cost reduction are judging which is more advantageous, A or B, and selecting which is most economical and advantageous among the several alternatives of A, B, C, and so on.

First let's consider judging. Frequently, problems arise when judging which of two things is better. For example, should a certain product be made internally or ordered from outside? In making a certain product, should we purchase machines exclusively for that purpose or use a general-purpose machine we already have?

We should not be biased in making such judgments. Take a cool look at the situation in your jurisdiction. Don't base judgments on a single cost analysis and conclude that it would be cheaper to order it from outside than to make it internally.

In selecting, we can consider many methods to achieve a manpower reduction. For example, we can buy automated machines, or change the work combination, or even consider buying robots. There are countless ways to achieve an objective when pursuing such improvement ideas. Therefore, we should list every conceivable improvement idea, examine each in depth, and, finally, select the best. If an improvement is pushed forward before thorough study, we can easily end up with an improvement that, while making a small cost reduction, costs too much to implement.

For example, let's suppose there is a suggestion to install a $500 electrical control device to replace one worker. If this $500 device could reduce the workforce by one worker, it would be a big gain for Toyota. If closer study reveals, however, that one worker could be eliminated at no cost by changing the sequence of work, then spending $500 would be considered a waste.

In Toyota's early days when buying automatic machines seemed so easy, such examples were numerous. This is a common problem for big as well as medium- and small-size businesses.

Toyota's main plant — its oldest facility — provides an example of a smooth production flow accomplished by re-arranging the conventional machines after a thorough study of the work sequence. The manager of a certain small business visited our main plant with the preconception that nothing would be relevant to his firm because Toyota was so much larger. Looking around the production plant, however, he realized that the old machines he had discarded long ago were working well at Toyota. He was amazed and thought we must have remodeled them.

It is crucial for the production plant to design a layout in which worker activities harmonize with rather than impede the production flow. We can achieve this by changing the work sequence in various ways. But if we rashly purchase the most advanced high-performance machine, the result will be overproduction and waste.

▶ Re-Examining the Wrongs of Waste

The Toyota production system is a method to thoroughly eliminate waste and enhance productivity. In production, "waste" refers to all elements of production that only increase cost without adding value — for example, excess people, inventory, and equipment.

Too many workers, equipment, and product only increase the cost and cause secondary waste. For example, with too many workers, unnecessary work is invented which, in turn, increases power and materials usage. This is secondary waste.

The greatest waste of all is excess inventory. If there is too much inventory for the plant to store, we must build a warehouse, hire workers to carry the goods to this warehouse, and probably buy a carrying cart for each worker.

In the warehouse, people would be needed for rust prevention and inventory management. Even then, some stored goods still rust and suffer damage. Because of this, additional workers will be needed to repair the goods before removal from the warehouse for use. Once stored in the warehouse, the goods must be inventoried regularly. This requires additional workers. When the situation reaches a certain level, some people consider buying computers for inventory control.

If inventory quantities are not completely controlled, shortages can arise. So despite planned daily production, some people will think shortages are a reflection on the production capacity. A plan for increasing production capacity is consequently put into the following year's equipment investment plan. With the purchase of this equipment, inventory increases even more.

The vicious cycle of waste generating waste hides everywhere in production. To avoid this, production managers and supervisors must understanding fully what waste is and its cause.

The above example is a worst-case scenario. Although I don't think this could happen in Toyota's production plant, similar phenomena might easily occur, although the extent would differ.

All of the primary and secondary wastes described above eventually become part of the direct and indirect labor cost, depreciation cost, and general management expenses. They would contribute to cost increases.

Considering these facts, we can never ignore the cost-raising elements. The waste caused by a single mistake will eat up the profit that ordinarily amounts to only a few percent of sales and thereby endanger the business itself. Behind the notion that the Toyota production system aims at reducing costs lies the above-mentioned understanding of the cost facts.

Eliminating waste is specifically aimed at reducing cost by reducing manpower and inventory, clarifying the extra availability of facilities and equipment, and gradually diminishing secondary waste. Regardless of how much is said, adopting the Toyota production system will be meaningless without a complete understanding of the elimination of waste. For this reason, I have explained it again.

▸ Generate Excess Capacity

I have mentioned that there are many ways to achieve a goal. Let's consider Toyota's thinking about what is economically advantageous from the standpoint of production capacity.

Opinions differ on the economic advantages of maintaining extra production capacity. In brief, excess capacity utilizes workers and machines that are otherwise idle, incurring no new expense. In other words, they cost nothing.

Let's consider excess capacity in internal versus external production. Often, cost comparisons are made between producing a product internally or ordering it from outside. If there is excess capacity for internal production, the only cost actually incurred is the variable expense that increases in proportion to the amount of production; for example, the material and oil cost. Consequently, without having to look at the cost comparison, internal production would be advantageous.

Now, consider the problem of waiting. If a worker has to wait until a pallet is full before transporting it, having him do line work or preparation would cost nothing. This point should require no study — it would be crazy to spend valuable time calculating the workpower.

Next is the problem of reducing lot sizes. When a general-purpose machine, such as a die press, has excess capacity, it is an advantage to reduce lot size as much as possible, aside from the separate problem of shortening setup time. If the machine still has excess capacity, it is better to continue reducing setup time to utilize it.

As we've seen above, when there is excess capacity, loss or gain is evident without requiring cost studies. The most important thing is to know the extent of excess capacity at all times. If we don't know whether there is excess capacity, we are bound to make mistakes in the selection process and incur expenses.

At Toyota, we go one step further and try to extract improvements from excess capacity. This is because, with greater production capacity, we don't need to fear new costs.

► The Significance of Understanding

In this section, I want to emphasize the importance of thoroughly understanding production and manpower reduction.

"The way we currently operate, the production line has a fairly high operation rate and fairly low defect rate. Therefore, as a whole, things seem to be proceeding reasonably."

If we allow ourselves to feel this way, we cut off any hope for progress or improvement.

"Understanding" is my favorite word. I believe it has a specific meaning — to approach an objective positively and comprehend its nature. Careful inspection of any production area reveals waste and room for improvement. No one can understand manufacturing by just walking through the work area and looking at it. We have to see each area's role and function in the overall picture. Through close observation, we can divide the movement of workers into waste and work:

- *Waste* — The needless, repetitious movement that must be eliminated immediately. For example, waiting for or stacking subassemblies.
- *Work* — The two types are non-value-added work and value-added work.

Non-value-added work may be regarded as waste in the conventional sense. For example, walking to pick up parts, opening the package of goods ordered from outside, operating the push buttons, and so forth are things that have to be done under present working conditions. To eliminate them, these conditions must be partially changed.

Value-added work means some kind of processing — changing the shape or character of a product or assembly. Processing adds value. In processing, in other words, the raw materials or parts are made into products to generate added value. The higher this ratio, the greater the working efficiency.

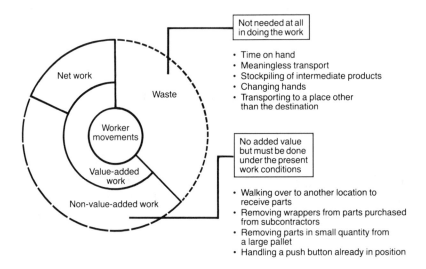

Figure 3. Understanding the Manufacturing Function

Examples of processing are: assembling parts, forging raw materials, press forging, welding, tempering gears, and painting bodies.

In addition, some production activities are outside the standard work procedures, for example, small repairs of equipment or tools and reworking defective products. Considering these, we come to realize that the ratio of value-added work is lower than most people think.

This is why I frequently emphasize that worker movement in the production area must be working, or value-adding movement. *Moving* is not necessarily working. Working means actually advancing the process toward completing the job. Workers must understand this.

Manpower reduction means raising the ratio of value-added work. The ideal is to have 100 percent value-added work. This has been my greatest concern while developing the Toyota production system.

► Utilizing the Full Work System

To raise the ratio of value-added work, we must be concerned with non-value-added movements, that is, the total elimination of waste. In connection with this problem, let's consider the redistribution of work.

If we see someone waiting or moving needlessly in a job done by a team of workers, it is not difficult to eliminate waste, redistribute the work load, and reduce manpower. In reality, however, such waste is usually hidden, making it difficult to eliminate. Let's look at some examples.

In any manufacturing situation, we frequently see people working ahead. Instead of waiting, the worker works on the next job, so the waiting is hidden. If this situation is repeated, inventory begins to accumulate at the end of a production line or between lines. This inventory has to be moved or neatly stacked. If these movements are regarded as "work," soon we will be unable to tell waste from work. In the Toyota production system, this phenomenon is called the waste of overproduction — our worst enemy — because it helps hide other wastes.

The most important step in reducing manpower is to eliminate overproduction and establish control measures. To implement the Toyota production system in your own business, there must be a total understanding of waste. Unless all sources of waste are detected and crushed, success will always be just a dream.

Let's look at one measure. With an automatic machine, suppose the standard inventory of a process is five pieces. If the inventory stands at only three pieces, the earlier process automatically starts producing the item until there are five pieces. When the inventory reaches its required number, the earlier process stops production.

If the standard inventory of the later process decreases by one, the earlier process starts production and sends the item to the later process. When the inventory in the later process reaches the required number, processing in the earlier process stops.

Thus, in such a system, standard inventories are always

maintained and the machines of each process work together to prevent overproduction. We call this the full work system.

▸ Do Not Make a False Show

To prevent overproduction and make items as needed, one by one, we have to know when they are needed. Thus, the appropriate tact time becomes important.

Tact is the length of time, in minutes and seconds, it takes to make one piece of the product. It must be calculated in reverse from the number of pieces to be produced. Tact is obtained by dividing the operable time per day by the required number per day (pieces). Operable time is the length of time that production can be carried out per day.

In the Toyota production system, we make a distinction between operating and operable rates. The *operating rate* means the present production record of a machine based on its full-time operation capacity. On the other hand, *operable rate* refers to the availability of a machine in operable condition when it is needed. The ideal operable rate is 100 percent. To achieve this, machine maintenance must be constant and setup times must be reduced.

For example, the operable rate of an automobile is the percentage of time the car will run smoothly when the driver wants it to — the ideal being, of course, 100 percent.

On the other hand, the operating rate refers to the amount of time per day the car is actually driven. Few people would drive a car any longer than needed. If one drove the car from morning till night regardless of need, the constant gasoline and oil consumption would increase the probability of mechanical problems and result in loss. Therefore, the ideal rate is not necessarily 100 percent.

To establish tact time, we must understand how the required production figures for the day are decided. But first, I would like to touch upon the relationship between production quantity and number of workers. If this relationship is viewed in terms of efficiency, we should remember that improving efficiency and reducing cost are not necessarily the same.

For example, on a production line, 10 workers produced 100 pieces of product per day. Improvements were introduced to increase efficiency. Now 10 workers could produce 120 pieces a day, a 20-percent increase in efficiency.

Demand rose at this time, so production could be increased to 120 pieces a day without having to increase manpower. Obviously, this cost reduction would increase profits.

Now, suppose that market demand — that is, the required number for production — drops to 100 or 90 pieces per day. What happens? If we continue to make 120 pieces a day because of our improved efficiency, we will have 20 to 30 pieces left over daily. This will increase our material and labor expenses and result in a serious inventory problem.

In a case like this, how can we improve efficiency and still reduce costs?

The problem is solved by improving the process so that eight workers can produce the daily required 100 pieces. If 90 pieces are needed, seven workers should be used. All of this requires that the process be improved.

At Toyota, increasing efficiency by increasing production while the actual demand or required number remains unchanged or even drops is called an "apparent increase [increase in calculation] of efficiency."

► Required Numbers Are All-Important

Required numbers are based on sales and this is determined by the market. Consequently, production is given a number based on demand or the actual orders — a number that cannot be increased or decreased arbitrarily.

Back in the days when you could sell everything you could make, people tended to forget about required numbers. They were busy buying high-performance machines that would allow them to keep up with the growing demand. Even while preparing for production increases, however, a business must also keep track of daily demand changes and be prepared with a system that can shift to reduced production when necessary. At Toyota, production has been built around required numbers.

As I described in the previous section, there are two ways to increase efficiency: (1) increase the production quantity or (2) reduce the number of workers.

If asked to choose between these methods, most people on the production line will tend toward increasing efficiency by increasing production. This is probably because reducing workers is more difficult and involves reorganizing the work-force. However, it is unrealistic not to reduce the number of workers if demand is dropping.

The goal, as I have often said, is cost reduction. Therefore, an increase in efficiency must be achieved by a method consistent with this goal. To eliminate overproduction reduce costs, it is absolutely necessary that the production quantity equal the required number.

Every Toyota plant produces in accordance with actual demand. Car dealers around the country send their orders daily to the main office of the Toyota Automobile Sales Company in Nagoya. These orders are classified by computer as to car type, model, fuel discharge rate, style, transmission, color, and so forth. The resulting data serve as the basis for production requirements at Toyota's production plants.

The production system itself is also based on this data. Increasing efficiency through manpower reduction can be realized only by eliminating waste from the tact time which is calculated from the required number. These improvements may enable a worker to do more or autonomate a portion of his or her work. The resulting extra manpower can then be utilized to carry out other production work. The operating rate of the machines is also determined this way.

▸ The Tortoise and the Hare

When thinking about overproduction, I often tell the story of the tortoise and the hare.

In a plant where required numbers actually dictate production, I like to point out that the slower but consistent tortoise causes less waste and is much more desirable than the speedy hare who races ahead and then stops occasionally to doze. The Toyota production system can be realized only when all the workers become tortoises.

High-performance machines were in demand for a long time before the term "high performance" was thoroughly examined. When we say high performance, we may mean high-precision finishing, low energy consumption, or even trouble-free machines. Each can be correct. However, a frequent mistake is to regard high-productivity and high-speed machines as being the same.

If we can raise the speed without lowering the operable rate or shortening the life of the equipment, if a higher speed will not change the manpower requirements or produce more products than we can sell — then we can say high speed means high productivity.

Speed is meaningless without continuity. Just remember the tortoise and the hare. Moreover, we cannot fail to notice that machines not designed for endurance at high speeds will have shortened lifespans if we speed them up.

Increasing speed in the name of productivity improvement alone or forcing high speeds on a machine that cannot endure them merely to avoid a drop in production may seem to benefit production. However, these actions actually hinder production. Production managers and supervisors as well as other managers must understand this.

► Take Good Care of Old Equipment

Does the value of equipment really go down? In the case of a worker, years of experience add depth and the worker's value to the company. A machine, lacking human qualities, is discarded after giving long service. I want to advocate that, like workers, machines that give long service should be used with great, great care.

The language of business economics talks of "depreciation," "residual value," or "book value" — artificial terms used for accounting, tax purposes, and convenience. Unfortunately, people seem to have forgotten that such terms have no relevance to the actual value of a machine.

For example, we often hear: "This machine has been depreciated and paid off, and, therefore, we can discard it any time without loss," or "The book value of this machine is zero. Why spend money on an overhaul when we can replace it with a new, advanced model?"

This kind of thinking is a big mistake.

If a piece of equipment purchased in the 1920s is kept up and can guarantee, at present, an operable rate close to 100 percent and if it can bear the production burden placed on it, the machine's value has not declined a bit. On the other hand, if a machine purchased last year has been poorly maintained and produces at only half its operable rate, we should regard its value as having declined 50 percent.

A machine's value is not determined by its years of service or its age. It is determined by the earning power it still retains.

When replacing old equipment, we can look at it economically in different ways. We can compare cost analyses or interest on investment. But can such methods that appear so logical really be used in a plant? We must not lose sight of the fact that these methods are based only on premise.

For example, some people think conventional maintenance is the only way. Then they decide that absolute loss can only be based on several premises. In practice, however, these methods cannot even be used as standards. Despite this, faced with a poorly maintained, deteriorating machine, they apply these methods and conclude it would be better to replace the machine. This is completely irrational.

How, then, should we decide whether or not to replace an old machine? My conclusion is that if adequate maintenance has been done, replacement with a new machine is never cheaper, even if maintaining the older one entails some expense. If we do decide to replace it, we should realize that we have either been misled by our calculations and made the wrong decision or that our maintenance program has been inadequate.

When we lose an economic argument, we then argue the validity of replacement by saying "it is too difficult to restore the needed precision" or "we want to overhaul it but have no substitute machine."

This reasoning is unsound. It shows we want new machines because we don't have a better idea. When replacing aged equipment, we should always decide case by case.

Whether overhauled or renewed, if the machines are poorly maintained and driven close to death, the costs incurred by replacement is enormous. Computed as maintenance cost, for example, it would mean nothing unless an actual effect was achieved in proportion to the cost increase.

► Look Straight at the Reality

Business management must be very realistic. A vision of the future is important but it must be down-to-earth. In this age, misreading reality and its ceaseless changes can result in an instant decline in business. We are indeed surrounded by a harsh environment.

Some people say the character of business must change. They insist that since our economic base has changed from high to low growth, we should repay loans and work only within the limits of working capital. We should have thought of this, however, in the high-growth period.

During high growth, such business changes might have been easy. But if one company increased production, others felt uneasy and so they also expanded. Machines and manpower were increased without questioning their efficiency. As a result, profits did not increase at the same rate sales did. Those satisfied with this reflected a "pre-management" mentality no longer acceptable in the business world's demanding environment.

A company prepared to carry out true rationalization while experiencing high growth could have held its growth to 5 percent and not increased equipment and workers. Other companies, meanwhile, would have expanded their sales by 10 percent. Doing so, profits might have increased enough to repay all the debts and expand the facilities. An action like this, from management's viewpoint, would have put business in a desirable position.

In the current low-growth period, market competition has become increasingly fierce — a battle of life and death. In such an environment, strengthening the character of business is an absolute requirement for survival.

In the effort to make the Toyota production system truly effective, there is a limit to what the Toyota Motor Company, a chassis maker, can do alone. Only by working as partners with the cooperating firms is it possible to perfect this system. The same is true in improving the character of management. Toyota alone cannot achieve the goal if the cooperating firms do not work together. So, we have been asking our cooperating firms to implement Toyota production system policies in their own businesses.

About 10 years ago, I visited the tempering shop of another company. At the time, our monthly production was approximately 70,000 cars.

The manager said, "We have enough manpower and equipment to cope with your order even if you make 100,000 cars."

So I asked him, "Then, is your plant closed for 10 days out of the month?"

He answered, "We would never do a silly thing like that."

Then I went to an earlier process — the machine processing section. There I saw women workers working like dogs at maximum speed because they did not want the furnace to be idle.

On calculation, the unit price was fairly low. The furnace in the tempering plant was filled with items to treat so that the fuel cost per unit would be less. Because they had the capacity to produce 100,000 car parts, they accumulated an extra 30,000 parts each month. Toyota was going to order only what we needed, however, so, the tempering firm probably had to build a warehouse.

The oil crisis made people begin to understand the waste of overproduction. And only then did they begin to recognize the Toyota production system's real value. I wish the readers could see for themselves how warehouses are disappearing one by one from the sites of our cooperating firms.

► 0.1 Worker Is Still One Worker

In business, we are always concerned with how to produce more with fewer workers.

In our company, we use the term "worker saving" instead of "labor saving." The term "labor saving" is somehow easily misused in a manufacturing company. Labor-saving equipment such as the lift and bulldozer, used mainly in construction work, are directly connected to reducing manpower.

In automobile plants, however, a more relevant problem is partial and localized automation. For example, in work involving several steps, an automatic device is installed only at the last stage. At other points in the operation, work continues to be done manually. I find this kind of labor saving all wrong. If automation is functioning well, that is fine. But if it is simply used to allow someone to take it easy, it is too costly.

How can we increase production with fewer workers? If we consider this question in terms of the number of worker days, it is a mistake. We should consider it in terms of number of workers. The reason is that the number of workers is not reduced even with a reduction of 0.9 worker days.

First, work and equipment improvement should be considered. Work improvement alone should contribute half or one-third of total cost reduction. Next, autonomation, or equipment improvement, should be considered. I repeat that we should be careful not to reverse work improvement and equipment improvement. If equipment improvement is done first, costs only go up — not down.

The company newspaper reported on a talk I gave on worker saving. In the story, the term "labor saving" was printed in error as "using fewer workers." But when I saw it, I thought, "This is true." "Using fewer workers" gets at the heart of the problem far better than "labor saving."

When we say "labor saving," it sounds bad because it implies eliminating a worker. Labor saving means, for example, a job that took 10 workers in the past is now done by eight workers — eliminating two people.

"Using fewer workers" can mean using five or even three workers depending on the production quantity — there is no fixed number. "Labor saving" suggests that a manager hires a lot of workers to start with, reducing the number when they are not needed. "Using fewer workers," by contrast, can also mean working with fewer workers from the start.

In actual experience, Toyota had a labor dispute in 1950 as a result of reducing its workforce. Immediately after its settlement, the Korean War broke out and brought special demands. We met these demands with just enough people and still increased production. This experience was valuable and, since then, we have been producing the same quantity as other companies but with 20 to 30 percent fewer workers.

How was this possible? In short, it was the effort, creativity, and power of its people that enabled Toyota to put into practice the methods that ultimately have become the Toyota production system. And this is not just an expression of conceit.

In the Toyota production system, we frequently say, "Do not make isolated islands." If workers are sparsely positioned here and there among the machines, it appears as if there are few workers. However, if a worker is alone, there can be no teamwork. Even if there is only enough work for one person, five or six workers should be grouped together to work as a team. By providing an environment sensitive to human needs, it becomes possible to realistically implement a system that employs fewer workers.

▸ Management by *Ninjutsu*

To think that mass-produced items are cheaper per unit is understandable — but wrong.

A company's balance sheet may regard work in process as having some added value and treat it as inventory or property. But this is where the confusion begins. Most of this inventory is frequently not needed and has no added value.

Increasing production is a prosperous business. Materials are purchased and workers work overtime. Even though the inventory they are generating is unnecessary, workers naturally demand overtime pay as well as a bonus.

We became accustomed to a working environment in which expanding sales and increasing capital, manpower, and machines were believed good. Management generally *did not see the forest for the trees.* And, naturally, business managers were mainly interested in their main motivation — profit.

These days we can make calculations too quickly, and this can cause problems. The following incident happened at the end of 1966 when we began producing the Corolla.

Corollas were fairly popular and selling well. We started with a plan to make 5,000 cars. I instructed the head of the engine section to make 5,000 units and use under 100 workers. After two or three months, he reported, "We can make 5,000 units with 80 workers."

After that, the Corolla kept selling well. So I asked him, "How many workers can make 10,000 units?"

He instantly answered, "160 workers."

So I yelled at him. "In grade school I was taught that two times eight equals sixteen. After all these years, do you think I should learn that from you? Do you think I'm a fool?"

Before long, 100 workers were making over 10,000 units. We might say mass production made this possible. But it was due largely to the Toyota production system in which waste, inconsistencies, and excesses were thoroughly eliminated.

I frequently say management should be done not by arithmetic but by *ninjutsu*, the art of invisibility. My meaning follows.

Other countries these days use the word "magic" in expressions like "management magic" or "management magician." In Japan, however, *ninjutsu* is more suitable for management. As children, we watched *ninjutsu* tricks at the movies — like the hero suddenly disappearing. As a management technique, however, it is something very rational.

To me, management by *ninjutsu* means acquiring management skills by training. In this age, I am painfully aware of the fact that people tend to forget the need for training. Of course, if skills to be learned are not creative or stimulating and if they do not require the best people, training may not seem worthwhile. But let's take a hard look at the world. No goal, regardless of how small, can be achieved without adequate training.

If in the United States there is management magic, then in Japan, we can call it the Toyota production system's management by *ninjutsu*, a reflection of its Japanese character and culture.

▶ In an Art Form, Action Is Required

If you look up the word "engineer" in an English dictionary, you might find "technologist," while in Japanese, its meaning uses the character for "art." Analyzing this character, you will find it is created by inserting the character "require" into the character "action." So, art seems to be something requiring action.

In mathematics, use of the abacus requires practice even though the principle of the abacus beads can be understood easily by anybody. But fast and accurate operation requires constant practice.

The martial art of *shinai*, the bamboo sword, was first called *gekken*, attacking with the sword. But it soon became *kenjutsu*, the art of using the sword. When actual fighting with the sword ceased in the beginning of the Meiji era, it became *kendō*, the way of the sword. Recently, it is being called *kengi*, the technique of using the sword.

In the era when the stronger opponent generally won, it was *gekken*, fighting with swords. But as the art form developed, even a weaker opponent could win and so it became *kenjutsu*. When the practical use of the sword was no longer in demand, it became *kendō*. In my opinion, swordsmanship advanced most during the *kenjutsu* era because action was required.

Action is also required in *gijutsu* (technology) — real action is what counts. The character for "talk" is also pronounced *jutsu*. Recently there seems to be more technology talk than practice. This should be a matter of great concern to us.

I feel that I am still a practicing technologist. I may not be a great speaker but it does not bother me. Talking about technology and actually practicing it are two different things. Computers began doing mathematics at the same time that *kenjutsu* changed from *kendō* to *kengi*. An art form has its own value, however, and I am still greatly attracted to it.

► Advocating Profit-Making Industrial Engineering

After World War II, the United States influenced Japan greatly in many ways. American cultural attitudes became fairly common nation-wide even in politics.

In the world of industry, America was, without dispute, the leader. Catching up with and surpassing America was not a job to be done in a day. To catch up, the shortest route was to buy advanced American technology. So, aggressive Japanese businesses imported and adopted America's high-level production and manufacturing technology. In academia and business, a great number of American business management techniques were also studied and discussed. For example, Japanese businesses carefully studied industrial engineering (IE), a company-wide manufacturing technology directly tied to management that was developed and applied in the United States.

Defining industrial engineering seems to be fairly difficult. When first introduced, it was pointed out that the Toyota production system was method engineering (ME), not IE. Don't be confused over the meanings.

To me, IE is not a partial production technology but rather a total manufacturing technology reaching the whole business organization. In other words, IE is a system and the Toyota production system may be regarded as Toyota-style IE.

What is the difference between traditional IE and the Toyota system? In brief, Toyota-style IE is *mōkeru* or profit-making IE, known as MIE. Unless IE results in cost reductions and profit increases, I think it is meaningless.

There are various definitions of IE. A former head of the American Steel Workers' Union defined its function as that of entering a plant to improve methods and procedures and to reduce costs. And this is exactly so.

"IE is the use of techniques and systems to improve the

method of manufacturing. In scope it ranges from work simplification to large-scale capital investment plans."[1]

"IE has two meanings. One aims at improving work methods in the plant or in a particular work activity. The other one means the specialized study of time and action. However, this is the work of a technician. Essentially, an industrial engineer studies systematic approaches to improvements."[2]

I would like to add a definition from the Society for Advancement of Management (SAM), an organization that succeeded the Taylor Society:

> Industrial engineering applies engineering knowledge and techniques for the study, improvement, planning, and implementation of the following:
>
> 1. method and system,
> 2. qualitative and quantitative planning and various standards including the various procedures in the organization of work,
> 3. measuring actual results under the standards and taking suitable actions.
>
> This is all done to exercise better management with special consideration for employee welfare, and it does not restrict business to lowering the cost of improved products and services.[3]

I have listed various IE definitions, each saying good things, because they are useful references. However, in private business, implementing IE effectively is not easy.

The reason I call Toyota's industrial engineering profit-making IE is my wish that the Toyota production system born and raised at Toyota Motor Company be comparable or superior to the American IE's business management and manufacturing system.

We are very happy that the Toyota production system has become, as I intended, a company-wide manufacturing technology directly tied to management. And, fortunately, it is extending to the outside cooperating firms as well.

► Surviving the Slow-Growth Economy

I have said before that I calmly accept the words "slow growth."

Over 5 percent macro-economic growth would be regarded as prosperity rather than recession, and we would consider 3 to 5 percent growth normal. Because future cycles may bring zero or negative growth, we must be prepared.

The Japanese automobile industry experienced negative growth immediately after the oil crisis and, at one time, fell into a slump. After that, however, exports improved and, compared to the sluggish state of other industries, the automobile industry alone seemed to enjoy good fortune. The actual situation, however, is not necessarily optimistic.

Domestic demand has matured following a cycle and, presently, a large demand cannot be hoped for. Export expansion will also slow down as a matter of course. In Europe and the United States, political and emotional resistance against Japanese cars has gradually risen. With the rising yen, the international market can also be expected to reflect a declining competitiveness of Japanese cars. Also, U.S. firms have entered into small-car manufacturing, negatively affecting Japanese exports.

The automobile industry may have been endowed with too much good fortune. There is already a hidden danger. If domestic demands continue their slow growth and if exports suffer even a slight slump, we shall face a serious situation.

Textile and utilities industries are regarded as economically depressed and it is said that the only formula for recovery lies in some basic business shifts. The automobile industry is presently booming, but there is no guarantee that it will not also fall on hard times.

In a severe recession or slow-growth economy, private enterprises must persevere by whatever means they can. The Toyota production system has been thorough in removing waste, inconsistency, and excess from production. It is by no means a passive or defensive management system.

The Toyota production system represents a revolution in thinking. Because it requires us to change our way of thinking in fundamental ways, I hear strong support as well as strong criticism. I find that the cause of such criticism is insufficient understanding of what the system is.

Of course, we have not made a big enough effort to teach people about the nature of the Toyota production system. However, it would not be an exaggeration to say that it has already gone beyond Toyota, the company, to become a uniquely Japanese production system.

4
▼

Genealogy of the
Toyota Production System

A Global World Around Us

IT IS SAID Toyoda Kiichirō once told Toyoda Eiji,[1] current president of Toyota, that in a comprehensive industry such as automobile manufacturing, the best way to work would be to have all the parts for assembly at the side of the line just in time for their use.

We have already called this idea of just-in-time the principle behind the Toyota production system. The words "just-in-time" pronounced by Toyoda Kiichirō were a revelation to some Toyota management people, one of whom became quite attached to the idea. And I have been attached ever since.

"Just-in-time" was new to us then and we found the concept stimulating. The idea of needed parts arriving at each process on the production line when and in the quantity needed was wonderful. Although it seemed to contain an element of fantasy, something made us think it would be difficult but not impossible to accomplish. In any case, it gave me an idea.

In the spring of 1932, I graduated from the mechanical technology department of Nagoya Technical High School and joined Toyoda Spinning and Weaving. The company was founded by Toyoda Sakichi, whom we might call the father of Toyota.

Two years earlier, the world saw New York's stock market crash. The ensuing worldwide economic depression still deeply affected the Japanese economy. Business was bad, unemployment was rising, the social atmosphere was violent and it was the year Prime Minister Inukai was assassinated.

My motive for joining Toyoda Spinning and Weaving was to use my technical education. Jobs were scarce at the time.

But my father, an acquaintance of Toyoda Kiichirō, helped me acquire a position.

I never dreamed of encountering Toyoda Kiichirō and the world of automobiles. But in 1942, Toyoda Spinning and Weaving was dissolved. In 1943, I was transferred to the Toyota Motor Company, where I entered Toyoda Kiichirō's busy realm of producing automobiles for the war effort.

My textile experience was valuable. Whether in car or fabric production, the relationship between workers and machines is basically the same. For a private business that is part of a secondary manufacturing industry, cost reduction remains management's biggest problem — in both the East and West.

Prior to the war and even the automobile, Japan's textile industry had been struggling in the rough waters of world trade. To catch up with and surpass Lancashire and Yorkshire, England's major textile regions, and to strengthen our international standing, we were already implementing cost reduction measures. Thus, Japan's textile industry already had a global view and was actively rationalizing its production methods.

In comparison, the automobile industry in Japan had a short history. Before and during World War II, Toyoda Kiichirō headed two teams of automobile engineers and business managers in an attempt to mass-produce cars domestically. But while truck production was reaching fairly high quantities, passenger car production was still far away.

By the late 1940s, Toyoda Kiichirō saw the possibility of his wish being fulfilled. In October 1949, the restriction on small passenger car production was lifted and price controls abolished. The lifting of distribution control and transition to independent sales came in April 1950. Unfortunately, at about this time, Toyoda Kiichirō resigned from the presidency, taking responsibility for the labor dispute.

Toyoda Spinning and Weaving and the Toyota Motor Company, while both small in scale, possessed a global atmosphere. When I joined Toyoda Spinning and Weaving in 1932, two years after Toyoda Sakichi's death, the legacy of the great inventor remained. Unconsciously, we seemed to know what "world class" was. Moving to the world of automobiles, I met Toyoda Kiichirō, whose foresight was matched by no one's. Thus, from the beginning, our corporate world was globally oriented.

▶ Two Extraordinary Characters

The two pillars of the Toyota production system are autonomation and just-in-time.

Autonomation was taken from the ideas and practice of Toyoda Sakichi. The Toyota-type auto-activated loom, which he invented, was fast as well as equipped with a device to automatically stop the machine should any one of the many warp threads break or the weft thread run out.

A major condition for production under the Toyota production system is the total elimination of waste, inconsistency, and excess. Therefore, it is essential that equipment be stopped immediately if there is a possibility of defects.

From Toyoda Sakichi, we learned that applying human intelligence to machines was the only way to make machines work for people. The following is an excerpt from an article by Haraguchi Akira entitled "Conversation with Toyoda Sakichi":

> The textile industry at that time was not as large as today's. Mostly, older women wove at home by hand. In my village, every family farmed and each house had a hand-weaving machine. Influenced by my environment, I gradually began thinking about this hand-weaving machine. Sometimes, I would spend all day watching the grandmother next door weaving. I came to understand the way the weaving machine worked. The woven cotton fabric was wound into a thicker and thicker roll. The more I watched, the more interested I became.

Toyoda Sakichi was talking about the spring of 1888 when he was 20 years old. Reading this, I was impressed by the way he observed all day, gradually understanding the way the loom operated and becoming more interested as he watched.

With any problem, I always ask *why* five times. This Toyota procedure is actually adapted from Toyoda Sakichi's habit of watching. We can talk about work improvement, but unless we know production thoroughly we can accomplish nothing. Stand on the production floor all day and watch — you will eventually discover what has to be done. I cannot emphasize this too much.

Opening our eyes and standing in the manufacturing plant, we really understand what waste is. We also discover ways to turn "moving" into "working," activities that always concern us.

"Just-in-time" came directly from Toyoda Kiichirō. This second Toyota pillar did not have the same objective as the auto-activated loom that prompted the idea of autonomation. It posed different sorts of difficulties.

Toyoda Sakichi went to America for the first time in 1910 when the automobile industry was just beginning. The popularity of cars was rising and many companies were attempting to produce them. Ford had been selling the Model T for two years when Toyoda Sakichi saw them in the marketplace.

Looking back, it must have been tremendously stimulating, especially to an inventor like Toyoda Sakichi. During his four months in America, he must have grasped what an automobile was and how it could become the feet of the people. On his return to Japan, he often said we were now in the era of automobiles.

In agreement with Toyoda Sakichi's wishes, Toyoda Kiichirō went into the business of cars. His understanding of the automobile industry and America's role was astute. He realized the great potential as well as the difficulty an automobile manufacturer would encounter dealing with countless peripheral firms and developing a compatible business system.

I was strongly affected by Toyoda Kiichirō's words: "just-in-time." Afterwards, I wondered about how he came up with the idea. Of course, I can never be positive because I couldn't ask him directly. But it is clear he thought a great deal about how to surpass America's highly developed automobile production system.

Just-in-time is a unique concept. Considering how difficult it is to understand even now, I cannot help paying respect to Toyoda Kiichirō's rich imagination.

► Learning from the Unyielding Spirit

Both Toyoda men had a strong, unyielding spirit. Toyoda Sakichi's was exposed, while Toyoda Kiichirō seems to have kept his hidden.

Statements made by Toyoda Sakichi between 1922 and 1924 strongly address the idea that Japanese people should challenge the world with their intelligence:

> Presently, white people question what contributions Japanese people have made to modern civilization. The Chinese invented the magnetic compass. But what invention did the Japanese make? Japanese people are merely imitators. This is what they say.
>
> Therefore, Japanese people must address this situation seriously. I am not saying to fight, but we must prove our intelligence and clear ourselves of this shame. ... Rather than stirring up hostility by competing internationally, we should progress enough to show our potential.
>
> We had Taka-Diastase[2] and Dr. Noguchi Hideyo.[3] But these achievements were made under the guidance of white people — with their help and the use of their facilities. I say we should achieve greatness through the capabilities of our own people, without assistance from outsiders.

In Toyoda Sakichi's statements we see a tremendous enthusiasm combined with insight. When Toyoda Kiichirō told us to catch up with America in three years, he did not show the same fighting spirit. However, his determination clearly reveals an aggressive nature. These two men are great leaders in Toyota history.

In November 1935, at the Toyota model car exhibition held in the Shibaura section of Tokyo, Toyoda Kiichirō repeated what his predecessor had once told him, "I served our country with the loom. I want you to serve it with the automobile." This was his dying wish and a story people still love to tell.

On March 26, 1952, a short time before Toyota's automobile enterprise went into full-scale operation, Toyoda Kiichirō passed away. It was indeed a great loss. I believe just-in-time was Toyoda Kiichirō's dying wish.

▸ Toyotaism with a Scientific and Rational Nature

"Toyotaism" was established by Toyoda Kiichirō. He placed the following conditions on the automobile business:

- To provide cars for the general public
- To perfect the passenger car industry
- To make reasonably priced cars
- To recognize the importance of sales in manufacturing
- To establish the basic material industry

Toyoda Kiichirō wrote an article, published in September 1936, entitled "Toyota to the Present" that provides a good description of Toyotaism. In the following excerpt, he makes some provocative points:

> At last, Toyota cars are out on the market. They are not here today because of a simple engineering hobby. The cars were born from the intense research of numerous people, a synthesis of ideas from different fields, and from dedicated efforts and countless failures over a long period of time.
>
> Would it be possible to make cars for the general population of Japan? Three years ago, many people would have said no. The most serious doubters were those experienced in automobile manufacturing.
>
> We started work early on engine design and research. Most preparation was finished in 1933, and on September 1, the tenth anniversary of the great earthquake,[4] we formally became an automobile production company.
>
> People called the venture reckless. We were warned how difficult it was to operate an automobile business. However, we had known this for several years and had worked hard to prepare ourselves. We firmly believed that Toyoda's strength and experience in automatic loom manufacturing would make our endeavor possible.
>
> Problems differed from those of weaving machines, however, and we realized the new business would be difficult to create. So, for three years we managed the business under the guise of a hobby.

But the unexpected lapse in automobile manufacturing forced us to take a business attitude — not a hobbyist's. The business now involves an obligation to the country. Whether we like it or not, we have to make it work as soon as possible.

Since formally deciding to go into car manufacturing, what have we done?... I will describe some of our preparations of the past three years.

The most important area in automobile manufacturing is, without a doubt, the problem of materials. To engage in car production without solving the materials problem is like building a house without a foundation.

In Japan, the steel industry is fairly advanced and can provide materials suited exclusively for automobiles. But turning steelmaking into a business would require a considerable investment as well as considerable research. No materials maker would be patient enough to provide the necessary assistance. And even if there were, they could not continue the necessary research indefinitely.

Materials progress means engine improvement. And progress in engine development means materials must be improved. To obtain the materials essential to engine research in Japan, we must manufacture them ourselves.

Regardless of how well an engine is made, its life will be short, its price high, and its performance poor if proper materials are not used at the right time. If we cannot make the materials, we cannot do the necessary research on the automobile. To do it would cost Japan over ¥2 million ($500,000).

Is it even possible for Japan to make the materials? The fastest way to get an answer was to ask Professor Honda Kōtarō.[5] So, I went to the city of Sendai and asked him. He said that, at present, Japan did have the capability and that there was no need to hire foreigners. Greatly relieved, I immediately set out to build a steel mill.

Some visitors to our company ask what percentage of our cast products pass the quality test. To sustain the business, 95 percent must pass. I felt that if we were in the sorry position of having to worry about the quality of our cast products, we might as well quit making cars. So, I encouraged our plant workers by saying it would be a shame for Toyota not to make its own cast products.

We failed many times before successfully blowing cylinders into the dies using die presses with a pass ratio of over 90 percent. We eventually succeeded, however, with the old die presses we had used with electric furnaces to cast thin parts for the looms. Even so, 500 to 600 cylinders were rejected.

After making 1,000 pieces of an item, most workers become fairly skilled and defect-free. But the first several 100 pieces will contain some good and some bad. Until skills are established, we have to be prepared to discard anything borderline. This is how materials problems are satisfactorily solved.

▸ Provide Good Equipment Even If the Factory Is Simple

Toyoda Kiichirō insisted on the highest quality equipment and worked to use them effectively:

We know machine manufacturing can be done using proper tools. But the problem is to produce them cheaply.

Machining cast products is not much different from manufacturing textile machines. Textile machines must be mass produced to a considerable extent. The same is true of automobiles. With textile machines, there are many varieties. In the case of the automobile, types may be fewer but greater accuracy and more specialized machines are necessary, such as fine boring and honing machines.

We can get ideas in other countries by studying the new manufacturing equipment being developed by other automotive machine makers. In this area, it is obvious that advanced equipment will enable us to make inexpensive products as good as those produced elsewhere.

Although I feel plant facilities can be as simple as barracks, I try to buy equipment that can perform perfectly — regardless of cost. We really have no alternative but to buy machines costing ¥50,000 ($12,500) to ¥60,000 ($15,000) each. If we are not prepared to spend money for good machines, we should not be in automobile manufacturing.

At the time, I tried to save money by using barracks as plants and reducing research spending. Regardless of how much I was laughed at, I would have run out of money had I continued buying things that were not needed. Eliminating a lot of small wastes enabled us to afford good equipment.

Machinery must be chosen carefully. To avoid ending up with wrong machines and wasting ¥30,000 ($7,500) to ¥50,000 ($12,500), we went to America to examine them first.

Once this expensive equipment is acquired, we have to learn to use it correctly. So, we study tool use because regardless of how good a machine is, we cannot produce large quantities accurately without proper tools. We need tools intended for mass production — and their design and production can easily take three to four years. This is what we have been doing since Toyota first bought the equipment three years ago.

After buying millions of yen worth of machinery, hundreds of people worked hard for three years without putting a single car on the market. Stockholders began to worry and wonder when cars would start rolling out. Those in charge also felt that somehow we should produce one or two cars just to show we were really doing something.

However, a car made this way would not be of the highest quality. This point is difficult for managers and capital investors to understand. If we hadn't had managers with enough courage to make a bold commitment to car manufacturing, we would not have found investors to trust the engineers and leave everything to them.

It would be easy if money was guaranteed once cars were produced. But money is always lost the first few years which is why this business is so difficult to establish. Anyone who plans such a endeavor and doesn't look ahead is foolish.

In the first few years, many managers thought this way. They considered me overly confident with no thought of the future.

It is easier to operate a tried and true business that uses known methods and will clearly make money. Starting a difficult business that no one else will touch is a challenge. But if it fails, the fault is entirely yours — and you can commit *harakiri* with a clear conscience.

I will go as far as I can with the automobile. If I do anything, it will be to make cars the public can afford. I know it will be difficult, but this is where I started.

▸ Pursuit of a Japanese-Style Production Technique

Toyoda Kiichirō's mission, while laying the foundation of the automobile business, was to develop a Japanese production technique. This required intelligence.

One reason it was difficult to develop an automobile industry in our country was that the car body could not be mass produced as in America. And it is difficult to establish the industry making car bodies by hand. This problem was always the most agonizing.

Someone suggested that we hire a foreigner. But that amounted to importing America's mass-production system and that didn't fit our situation. At the time, we lacked almost everything pertaining to this industry and were actually making parts by hand.

Japanese people are by nature craft-oriented and make many things by hand. Mass production, however, requires using die presses. But we were not going to make tens of millions of cars as in America, and we could not invest as much money to make dies. Somehow, we had to combine the die presses and hand-finishing in a way that avoided copying the American method exactly.

I had to thoroughly examine the industry to see how far it had advanced. So I toured the plants in the Tokyo area with the guidance of Kawamata Kazuo. On a tour of Sugiyama Steel where they were making fenders with die presses, I received some unexpected help.

There could have been other plants doing similar work but I asked Mr. Sugiyama if he would be interested in making the mold for the car body. He said yes. Because it was the first time and we had no equipment that could do it, we studied various methods and did the finishing by hand.

Other countries, of course, have machines for making molds. Some manufacturers specialize in making models for different companies and, unlike Japan, can afford to install thousands of such machines. Because hand-finishing would be faster and less costly, however, we decided to handcraft it this time and produce a rough mold in about a year and a half. This area needs future research.

The next point is that top-grade sheet metal greatly facilitates making the molds for the die presses. We asked Professor Mishima Tokushichi to study sheet metal. During a foreign tour, he learned some advanced techniques that will enable us to greatly improve our products. We are experienced in coating and lining and will require no assistance in those areas.

Lastly, in assembly, we need equipment, setups, and skill in the assembly area. Japanese people are adept with their hands and training will be no problem. In the near future, I am certain we can make better cars for less than foreign manufacturers.

► Making Products That Have Value

With the May 1936 enactment of the automobile manufacturing business law, domestic car manufacturers came under government protection and assistance. Under this law, business in the automobile industry required a government permit and the domestic automobile industry's growth was to be protected by suppressing the foreign car assembly businesses. This was a powerful government protectionist policy.[6]

However, Toyoda Kiichirō recognized that the market always demands reasonably priced products. Although he believed the legislation would prevent wild competition, he feared that, if relied on too heavily, it would eventually force customers to abandon the domestic industry. As a personal warning, his writings reveal his concern for self-responsibility on private business.

Using our present knowledge, we can at least make the shape of an automobile. Future progress will depend on academic research. Today's problem, however, is that, regardless of how good a car we make, it will mean nothing unless we make it economically.

This problem eventually relates to price. What quantity must we produce in Japan to enable us to sell domestic cars at reasonable prices? No one can know this figure with certainty.

Cars have to be sold at prices that are reasonable today. But what is reasonable? We know our cars will not sell unless they are cheaper than foreign models. We might manage to sell 50 to 100 cars a month by appealing to patriotism. But selling 200 or 500 would be difficult. In the end, prices must be competitive. A consumer automatically derives pleasure from buying something at a lower price.

We know from experience in purchasing equipment that prices are sometimes driven down more than necessary. Cars sold to government agencies may bring the desired price, but in other cases prices must be lowered. Appealing to patriotism here would be useless. If prices are not kept low, we will be unable to sell hundreds of cars a month.

Good marketing and skillful advertising might allow us to deceive the buyers for a while — but not for long. As people learn the value of domestic cars, they will buy only if the price is commensurate. They won't buy just for the sake of the country.

It is a new product and we must invest the money to produce it well and keep prices low. To make and sell cars domestically, manufacturers must carefully consider whether or not they can make ends meet with such prices.

Fortunately, the automobile manufacturing business legislation has been enforced to a certain extent. However, if it increases the price of both foreign and domestic cars, we will have only ourselves to blame. The law should enable domestic car production to improve so that consumers can pay less. On this point, we have a great responsibility, but, at the same time, we cannot offer low prices at the beginning.

Can we actually produce economical cars domestically? Low prices are fine — but if they mean poor materials, poor quality, and eventually unusable products, nothing is achieved. How do we break through this dilemma? The automobile manufacturing business law would be useful in reducing the pressure of competition, especially the dumping practices of the well-established foreign companies. But, in fair competition, we must rely on our own capability.

▸ A Chessplayer's View

Toyoda Sakichi and Toyoda Kiichirō had an international business perspective and excelled at perceiving the world as a whole. They had the foresight to go always to the heart of the matter. Both spent their lives mainly in the production fields, looking at things realistically, calmly, and objectively.

A person standing in a production area can end up cleaning the corner of an enormous box with a toothbrush. Toyoda

Sakichi and Toyoda Kiichirō were different and always studied the entire picture. They had the overview of chessplayers and were constantly designing strategies. They knew how to checkmate.

In Haraguchi Akira's interview, we discover that Toyoda Sakichi was an inventor of great genius:

> He would not read catalogues or books. He would not borrow from newspapers or magazines. He never asked for information or borrowed from others to help in an invention. He never studied mathematics or physics. His thinking and inventing were accomplished completely by himself. No mathematics teacher or mechanical expert could find fault with his inventions. His logic fit all scientific principles.
>
> Because his inventions sprang directly from actual practice, they did not always follow scientific principles. In application, however, his inventions produced better results. He put his ideas into actions, not words.
>
> He didn't use consultants or assistants. He was independent and alone. He did not have a special research lab or any reference materials at his side. The living room in his home was his laboratory and office. He had no visitors and he wouldn't call on anyone. From morning till night, he would sit in the room, looking up at the ceiling and down at the surface of the mattress, pondering things quietly. In this way, he generated over one hundred patents.

Find a subject to think about, stare at an object until a hole is almost bored through it, and find out its essential nature. Stand and watch a neighborhood grandmother's hand loom for a whole day. This was how Toyoda Sakichi was inspired and tracked down the facts.

He went abroad to make first-hand observations. We cannot help but be impressed by his progressive nature. He would expand an idea to its fullest capacity and, the next moment, compress it to its smallest form. In terms of chess, he had both an overall view of the chessboard as well as checkmating capability.

In 1911, Toyoda Sakichi toured Europe and the United States. Prior to that, under adverse and complicated circumstances, he quit the Toyoda Spinning and Weaving Company. But in America, when he saw the Northrop and Ideal

System automatic looms, deemed the period's outstanding achievements, he recognized the superiority of his own inventions. Thus, after traveling abroad, he re-established himself and again demonstrated his unyielding spirit.

At that time in America, he also saw cars. He decided at once to go into automobile manufacturing after the automatic loom. In his mind, his looms and the automobile were strongly connected.

Toyoda Sakichi's auto-activated loom and the ring-type loom, had things in common with automobiles. Both functioned automatically using machine power. Also, in terms of idea and application, the ring-type loom overcoming the limitation of thread length in textile making was similar to the unlimited nature of an automobile running freely on a road without tracks.

Toyoda Sakichi's imagination, although boundless, was always realistic. Returning from America, he is said to have announced, "From now on, it's the automobile." Thus, in his mind, besides looms, a chessplayer's view of the Japanese automobile industry was forming.

▸ In Search of Something Japanese

The path from Toyoda Sakichi to Toyoda Kiichirō and then to the present Toyota Motor Company is the path of a developing and maturing modern Japanese industry. The line connecting them is the pursuit of a technology of Japanese origin.

In 1901, Toyoda Sakichi first thought about inventing an auto-activated loom. Twenty-five developmental years later, it was accomplished entirely by Japanese people. This was Toyoda Sakichi's wish and it was fulfilled.

Going through his records, we find a fierce, challenging attitude toward Europeans, a sense of rivalry. He himself stated that it was an intelligent rivalry, a perception that was ahead of his time.

Toyoda Sakichi's mission in life, business, and the world was to cultivate and train the natural intellect of the Japanese people, sell original Japanese products produced by this intellect, and increase the national wealth of Japan.

Toyoda Sakichi sold his own cultivated intellect in the form of his patents. Today we might call the development and production of Toyoda Sakichi's auto-activated loom a high-density, "how-to" industry.

Platt Brothers of England purchased the patent for the loom in 1930. It is a well-known story that the ¥1 million ($500,000) that resulted from this deal was spent on automobile research.

I am overwhelmed by Toyoda Sakichi's tenacity in employing the Japanese intellect he regarded so highly. He believed Japanese business as well as the country would continue to lag behind the European-American world unless the creativity and original technology of Japanese people was discovered. Raising this national consciousness became his personal goal.

Japan's role in today's world of buying and selling commodities is very large. Actually, the role is sometimes too large and causes friction. Overcoming this problem will require politically facilitated agreements regarding quantities. When I think in purely economic terms, I conclude that we must export commodities with high added value that are marketable domestically as well. This means commodities demanding a lot of brain power, as Toyoda Sakichi used to say. Eventually, we may have to export intellect itself.

Toyoda Sakichi pursued and developed an original Japanese technology. I know no better example than Toyoda Sakichi, who did not confine himself to an ivory tower, but discovered things to study in real life, inventing and commercializing the auto-activated loom that attained the world's highest level of mechanical design and performance. Although many great ideas emerge from the academic world, few inventions are born in industry or become the organizing principle of the industry itself. In Japan, especially, such examples are rare.

Taka-Diastase developed by Dr. Takamine Jōkichi was obviously a Japanese creation, as Toyoda Sakichi pointed out, but the work was done in a foreign laboratory. Although this does not lower its value, it does distinguish it from Toyoda

Sakichi's invention in how and where it was achieved. There were as yet few Japanese scientific achievements, and the soil to grow such achievements was not very fertile. For this reason, Toyoda Sakichi's achievements were unique.

Touching upon Toyoda Kiichirō's keen insight, in his article "Toyota to the Present" cited earlier, he said the quality of the sheet metal in the die presses greatly affects the making of the mold. It is much easier to make molds using top-grade sheeting. Dr. Mishima Tokushichi was asked to study this issue.

MK steel, invented by Dr. Mishima, was one of the few Japanese discoveries along with the ferrite or NKS magnet invented by Dr. Honda Kōtarō. Toyoda Kiichirō's expectations were extremely high. Unfortunately, the German Bosch Company and General Electric of the United States made greater efforts to apply these inventions. Nonetheless, Toyoda Kiichirō watched them more carefully than other Japanese businessmen.

At every opportunity, Toyoda Kiichirō emphasized the importance of cooperation between academia and industry in establishing businesses like automobile manufacturing. He felt that, in everything, a strong foundation was essential.

▸ Witnessing a Dialectic Evolution

Before his involvement with automobiles, Toyoda Kiichirō worked with weaving machines. Many of our elders helped Toyoda Sakichi with his great invention, putting it to work in the business. They worked behind the scenes, unknown to the outside world. In the early days, Toyoda Kiichirō worked busily at Toyoda Sakichi's feet developing and commercializing the automatic looms, selling them to foreign businesses, and negotiating contracts, and so forth.

Although interested in automobiles from the start, it was perhaps during his tour of Europe and America in 1930, when he went to England to negotiate with Platt Brothers, that he was most strongly influenced. New York especially must have shocked him with its flood of cars.

When Toyoda Kiichiro returned home, the bedridden Toyoda Sakichi asked him to report in detail on the automobile situation in the United States and Europe. Then, Toyoda Sakichi instructed him to spend the ¥1 million from Platt Brothers on automobile research, an amazing act of courage and foresight. Toyoda Kiichiro must have been filled with tremendous excitement and a sense of responsibility when he received the instructions.

I look at the changes in the period from Toyoda Sakichi to Toyoda Kiichiro as a time of evolution. In the same sense, I look at the changes from Toyoda Kiichiro to the present time as a similar and continuing evolution. In this evolution, there are mountains and valleys. There are successes and failures. There are favorable and adverse situations. There is movement and stagnation. The flow of a stream is sometimes rapid and sometimes slow and sometimes the stream seems to be drying up.

In Toyota's evolution, something in the stream has been continual, solid, and based on Japanese creativity. Toyoda Kiichiro realized better than anyone else that things cannot be achieved in a day. He was eager to learn the basics of automobile manufacturing as quickly as possible from General Motors and Ford. He acquired materials from the American producers to compare with those of Japan and then looked for a Japanese method of production.

In 1933, Toyoda Kiichiro announced the goal to develop domestically produced cars for the general public:

"We shall learn production techniques from the American method of mass production. But we will not copy it as is. We shall use our own research and creativity to develop a production method that suits our own country's situation."

I believe this was the origin of Toyoda Kiichiro's idea of just-in-time.

True innovation — I mean real technological innovation — also brings some kind of social reform. Like Ford's Model A, Toyoda Sakichi's auto-activated loom also brought an industrial revolution.

The world of the automobile that Toyoda Kiichirō entered was, in a broad sense, a composite industry. To narrow the gap between the Japanese and American automobile industries and create a domestic production system, he had to explore ways to learn the basic technology, master the different production technologies, organize the production system, and find a uniquely Japanese production technology.

Thus, Toyoda Kiichirō must have clearly envisioned just-in-time as the first step in the evolution of a Japanese production system. It is, in fact, the starting point of the Toyota production system, constituting its skeletal structure. We can see, therefore, how the search for Japanese originality flows into the creative development of the Toyota system.

From Toyoda Sakichi to Toyoda Kiichirō to the present, Toyota as a company has managed to evolve in the midst of enormous internal and external changes, a process that might be called a dialectic evolution.

The True Intention of the Ford System

The Ford System and the Toyota System

HENRY FORD (1863-1947), without dispute, created the automobile production system.

Strictly speaking, there may be as many ways of making automobiles as there are automobile companies or individual manufacturing plants. This is because production methods reflect the philosophy of business management and the individuality of the person in charge of the plant. However, the basis of automobile production as a modern industry is the mass-production system that Ford himself practiced.

The Ford system symbolizes mass production and sales in America even today. It is a mass-production system based on work flow, sometimes called the automation system.

This is the real mass production system in which raw materials are machined and carried along conveyor belts to be transformed into assembled parts. The components of various types are then supplied to each of the final assembly processes, with the assembly line itself moving at a fixed speed, as parts are assembled to ultimately become fully assembled cars coming off the line one by one.

To clarify the difference between the Ford and Toyota production systems, let's first take a close look at the Ford system.

Charles E. Sorensen, the Ford Company's first president, originally headed production and was, therefore, an important man in Ford history. His book, *My Forty Years with Ford*, bestows advice and describes the history of Ford's development. The following excerpt vividly portrays the beginning and evolution of the Ford system:

As may be imagined, the job of putting the car together was a simpler one than handling the materials that had to be brought to it. Charlie Lewis, the youngest and most aggressive of our assembly foremen, and I tackled the problem. We gradually worked it out by bringing up only what we termed the fast-moving materials. The main bulky parts, like engines and axles, needed a lot of room. To give them that space, we left the smaller, more compact, light-handling material in a storage building on the northwest corner of the grounds. Then we arranged with the stock department to bring up at regular hours such divisions of material as we had marked out and packaged.

This simplification of handling cleaned things up materially. But at best, I did not like it. *It was then that the idea occurred to me that assembly would be easier, simpler, and faster if we moved the chassis along, beginning at one end of the plant with a frame and adding the axles and the wheels; then moving it past the stockroom, instead of moving the stockroom to the chassis.* I had Lewis arrange the materials on the floor so that what was needed at the start of assembly would be at that end of the building and the other parts would be along the line as we moved the chassis along. We spent every Sunday during July planning this. Then one Sunday morning, after the stock was laid out in this fashion, Lewis and I and a couple of helpers put together the first car, I'm sure, that was ever built on a moving line.

We did this simply by putting the frame on skids, hitching a towrope to the front end and pulling the frame along until axles and wheels were put on. Then we rolled the chassis along in notches to prove what could be done. While demonstrating this moving line, we worked on some of the subassemblies, such as completing a radiator with all its hose fittings so that we could place it very quickly on the chassis. We also did this with the dash and mounted the steering gear and the spark coil.[1]

This describes the scene of the first experiment in setting up the work flow at Ford. The basic form of this work flow is common to all automobile businesses around the world. Even though today, some manufacturers — Volvo, for instance — have one person assemble the entire engine, in general, the manufacturing mainstream still utilizes Ford's work flow, or automation, system. Although the events described by Sorensen took place around 1910, the basic pattern has changed very little.

Like Ford's, the Toyota production system is based on the work flow system. The difference is that, while Sorensen worried about warehousing parts, Toyota eliminated the warehouse.

► Small Lot Sizes and Quick Setup

Making large lots of a single part — that is, punching out a large quantity of parts without a die change — is a common-sense production rule even today. This is the key to Ford's mass production system. The American automobile business has continuously shown that planned mass production has the greatest effect on cost reduction.

The Toyota system takes the reverse course. Our production slogan is "small lot sizes and quick setups." Why are we so different from — in fact, the opposite of — the Ford system?

For example, the Ford system promotes large lot sizes, handles vast quantities, and produces lots of inventory. In contrast, the Toyota system works on the premise of totally eliminating the overproduction generated by inventory and costs related to workers, land, and facilities needed for managing inventory. To achieve this, we practice the kanban system in which a later process goes to an earlier process to withdraw parts needed just in time.

To make certain the earlier process produces only as many parts as are picked up by the later process, the workers and equipment in each production process must be able to produce the number of parts required when they are needed. If the later process varies its pick-up in terms of time and amount, however, the earlier process must be prepared to have available the maximum amount possibly needed in the fluctuating situation. This is an obvious waste that boosts costs.

Complete elimination of waste is the basis of the Toyota production system. Therefore, production leveling is strictly practiced and fluctuation is flattened or smoothed. Lot sizes are made smaller and the continuous flow of one item in large quantity is avoided.

For example, we do not consolidate all Corona production in the morning and Carina production in the afternoon. Coronas and Carinas are always produced in an alternating sequence.

In short, where the Ford system sticks to the idea of making a quantity of the same item at one time, the Toyota system synchronizes production of each unit. The idea behind this approach is that in the marketplace, each customer buys a different car, so in manufacturing, cars should be made one at a time. Even at the stage of making parts, production is carried out one piece at a time.

To be able to average production and reduce lot sizes, quick die changes are necessary. In the 1940s, in Toyota's production department, setups in large processes took two to three hours. So, for efficiency and economy, die changes were avoided as much as possible. At first, the idea of quick setup met strong resistance in the production area.

Setup was regarded as an element that reduces efficiency and increases cost — and there seemed no reason for workers to want to change dies cheerfully. On this point, however, we had to ask them to change their attitude. Rapid changeovers are an absolute requirement for the Toyota production system. Teaching workers to reduce lot sizes and setup times took repeated on-the-job training.

In the 1950s, when production leveling was being pushed at Toyota, setup time was reduced to under an hour, sometimes dropping to 15 minutes. This is an example of training workers to meet needs by changing what is considered to be common sense.

General Motors, Ford, and the European automobile makers have been improving and refining production processes in their own way. They have not attempted, however, the production leveling Toyota has been working to achieve.

Using a large die press as an example, European and American manufacturers still take a long time for setup — perhaps because there is no need to hurry. Nevertheless, lot sizes remain large and they continue to pursue mass production under a planned production system.

Which is in the superior position, the Ford system or the Toyota system? Because each is undergoing daily improvement and innovation, a quick conclusion cannot be drawn. I firmly believe, however, that as a production method the Toyota system is better suited to periods of low growth.

▸ The Foresight of Henry Ford

Sorensen writes that Henry Ford was not the father — but a sponsor of the mass-production system. Not everyone would agree on this point. I, for one, am in awe of Ford's greatness. I think that if the American king of cars were still alive, he would be headed in the same direction as Toyota.

I believe Ford was a born rationalist — and I feel more so every time I read his writings. He had a deliberate and scientific way of thinking about industry in America. For example, on the issues of standardization and the nature of waste in business, Ford's perception of things was orthodox and universal.

The following excerpt from Ford's book, *Today and Tomorrow*,[2] reveals his philosophy of industry. It is from a chapter entitled "Learning from Waste":

> Conserving our natural resources by withdrawing them from use is not a service to the community. That is holding to the old theory that a thing is more important than a man. Our natural resources are ample for all our present needs. We do not have to bother about them as resources. What we do have to bother about is the waste of human labour.
>
> Take a vein of coal in a mine. As long as it remains in the mine, it is of no importance, but when a chunk of that coal has been mined and set down in Detroit, it becomes a thing of importance, because then it represents a certain amount of the labour of men used in its mining and transportation. If we waste that bit of coal — which is another way of saying if we do not put it to its full value — then we waste the time and energy of men. A man cannot be paid much for producing something which is to be wasted.
>
> My theory of waste goes back of the thing itself into the labour of producing it. We want to get full value out of labour so that we may be able to pay it full value. It is use — not conservation — that interests us. We want to use material to its utmost in order that the time of men may not be lost. Material costs mean nothing.

It is of no account until it comes into the hands of management.

Saving material because it is material, and saving material because it represents labour might seem to amount to the same thing. But the approach makes a deal of difference. We will use material more carefully if we think of it as labour. For instance, we will not so lightly waste material simply because we can reclaim it — for salvage involves labour. The ideal is to have nothing to salvage.

We have a large salvage department, which apparently earns for us twenty or more million dollars a year. Something of it will be told later in this chapter. But as that department grew and became more important and more strikingly valuable, we began to ask ourselves:

Why should we have so much to salvage? Are we not giving more attention to reclaiming than to not wasting?

And with that thought in mind, we set out to examine all our processes. A little of what we do in the way of saving manpower by extending machinery has already been told, and what we are doing with coal, wood, power and transportation will be told in later chapters. This has to do only with what was waste. Our studies and investigations up to date have resulted in the saving of 80,000,000 pounds of steel a year that formerly went into scrap and had to be reworked with the expenditure of labour. This amounts to about three million dollars a year, or, to put it in a better way, to the unnecessary labour on our scale of wages of upward of two thousand men. And all of that saving was accomplished so simply that our present wonder is why we did not do it before.[3]

▸ Standards Are Something to Set Up Yourself

In 1937 or 1938, while still working at Toyoda Spinning and Weaving, I was once told by my boss to prepare a standard work sheet for weaving. As I mentioned earlier, I found it very difficult. Since then, I have continued to think about what is meant by the word "standard" in standard work.

The elements to consider in standard work are worker, machine, and materials. If not combined effectively, the workers will feel alienated and find it impossible to produce efficiently.

Standards should not be forced down from above but rather set by production workers themselves. Only when the plant system is considered as a whole can standards for each production department become defect-free and flexible.

In this sense, standards should be thought of not only as the production department's standards but also as top management's. Let us hear Ford's opinion in his chapter on standards in *Today and Tomorrow*:

> One has to go rather slowly on fixing standards, for it is considerably easier to fix a wrong standard than a right one. There is the standardizing which marks inertia, and the standardizing which marks progress. Therein lies the danger in loosely talking about standardization.
>
> There are two points of view — the producer's and the consumer's. Suppose, for instance, a committee or a department of the government examined each section of industry to discover how many styles and varieties of the same thing were being produced, and then eliminated what they believed to be useless duplication and set up what might be called standards. Would the public benefit? Not in the least — excepting in war time, when the whole nation has to be considered as a production unit. In the first place, no body of men could possibly have the knowledge to set up standards, for that knowledge must come from the inside of each manufacturing unit and not at all from the outside. In the second place, presuming that they did have the knowledge, then these standards, although perhaps effecting a transient economy, would in the end bar progress, because manufacturers would be satisfied to make the standards instead of making to the public, and human ingenuity would be dulled instead of sharpened.[4]

We see in Ford's thinking his strong belief that a standard is something not to be directed from above. Whether it be the federal government, top management, or a plant manager, the person who establishes the standard should be someone who works in production. Otherwise, Ford emphasizes, the standard would not lead to progress. And I agree.

In pursuing the definition of standards, Ford's thinking extends into the future of private businesses and industry:

> The eventuality of industry is not a standardized, automatic world in which people will not need brains. The eventuality is a

world in which people will have a chance to use their brains, for they will not be occupied from early morning until late at night with the business of gaining a livelihood. The true end of industry is not the bringing of people into one mould; it is not the elevating of the working man to a false position of supremacy — industry exists to serve the public of which the working man is a part. The true end of industry is to liberate mind and body from the drudgery of existence by filling the world with well-made, low-priced products. How far these products may be standardized is a question, not for the state, but for the individual manufacturer.[5]

Here, the foresight of Ford is revealed clearly. We see that automation and the work-flow system invented and developed by Ford and his collaborators were never intended to cause workers to work harder and harder, to feel driven by their machines and alienated from their work. As in everything else, however, regardless of good intentions, an idea does not always evolve in the direction hoped for by its creator.

Tracing the conception and evolution of work flow by Ford and his associates, I think their true intention was to extend a work flow from the final assembly line to all other processes; that is, from machine processing to the die press that corresponds to the earlier processes in our Toyota system.

By setting up a flow connecting not only the final assembly line but all the processes, one reduces production lead time. Perhaps Ford envisioned such a situation when he used the word "synchronization."

Ford's successors, however, did not make production flow as Ford intended. They ended up with the concept "the larger the lot size, the better." This builds a dam, so to speak, and stops the flow at the machining and stamping processes.

As I already mentioned, American-style labor unions may also have hindered the work flexibility in the production area, but I do not think this was the only cause. A major reason is that Ford's successors misinterpreted the work flow system. The final process is indeed a work flow, but in other production lines, I think they were forcing the work to flow.

In the course of developing the Toyota production system — changing from a forced to a real work flow — human intelligence was transferred to countless machines. In this way, the two pillars, just-in-time and autonomation, were both the means of realizing the system as well as the end.

▸ Prevention Is Better than Healing

To prepare for future natural disasters, people are accustomed to stockpiling goods, for example, the Japanese farming tribes. Although not necessarily a bad social custom, I deny its value in industry. I am talking about the way today's managers store raw materials and finished products to meet unexpected demands.

Business is connected to the outside world. Why, then, should it store things for its own safety? As I have often said, this tendency to store things is the start of waste in business.

"If a new machine is purchased, keep it operating full-time... As long as it is running smoothly, let the machine produce to capacity... In case of future trouble with the machine, let it produce while it can." This way of thinking is still deeply rooted among manufacturing people.

In an era of low growth, such ideas no longer apply, but the tendency to make and store is still strong. If Toyota's just-in-time principle works, certainly there is no need for storing extra raw materials and finished products.

But what should we do if the machine stops and production requirements cannot be met? Under the kanban system, what would happen if the later process went to the earlier process to pick up needed goods and found the machine down and the goods not produced? Certainly, it would be a difficult situation.

For this reason, the Toyota production system stresses in all production processes the need for prevention. If we think to keep inventory in anticipation of machine problems, why not consider preventing trouble before it occurs?

As the Toyota production system gradually spread within and outside the Toyota Motor Company, I asked everyone concerned to study how machine problems and process difficulties could be prevented. Thus, preventive "medicine" or maintenance became an integral part of the Toyota production system.

Ford had similar ideas on this subject. To fulfill his business's social responsibility, he established hospitals, schools, and the well-known Ford Foundation. When a hospital was built, Ford published his opinions on health, disease, treatment, and prevention.

In a chapter entitled "Curing or Preventing," Ford argues that if we can find good food and prepare it perfectly, health can be maintained and disease prevented:

> The best doctors seem to agree that the cure for most indispositions is to be found in diet and not in medicine. Why not prevent that illness in the first place? It all leads up to this — if bad food causes illness, then the perfect food will cause health. And that being the case, we ought to search for that perfect food — and find it. When we have found it, the world will have taken its greatest single step forward.[6]

Ford pointed out that the possibility of succeeding in this crucial goal would be greater if its scientific study was organized not by a research institution but by business as a socio-business need. While he did not say prevention itself was indispensable to the work flow that forms the basis of the Ford system, it is interesting to discover that the man who invented automation also pondered such problems.

A strong production line means a strong business. In describing the complementary relationship between just-in-time and autonomation, Toyota's two supporting pillars, I emphasize their part in building a production line with a strong constitution. Toyota's strength does not come from its healing processes — it comes from preventive maintenance.

▸ Is There a Ford after Ford?

I have been talking about the origins of the Ford system, the mass-production system presently dominating the United States.

With respect to work flow, Toyota has learned a lot from the Ford system. The Ford system was born in America, however, and ushered in the automobile age with its introduction of the mass-produced Model T. I have similarly sought a Japanese-style production system equally suited to the environment of Japan.

As to the evolution of the Ford automation system in American automobile manufacturing, the Ford Company included, I think Ford's true intention has not been accurately understood. As I have already said, the reason I think this is that, compared to the smooth flow in an automobile plant's final assembly line, the flow of other processes has not been established and a system based on large lots that seem to stop the flow has been incorporated.

Why is this? Before Ford's ultimate goal was understood clearly, competition in the U.S. automobile marketplace intensified. The Ford Company itself was under pressure from its rival, General Motors. I think this situation halted study of the appropriate development of the Ford system.

The fact that the American automobile industry faced a major turning point in the 1920s is well described in the book *My Years with General Motors*, written by Alfred P. Sloan, Jr., the former Chairman of the Board of General Motors.

According to Sloan, an incident occurred between 1924 and 1926 that changed America's automobile industry dramatically. The smaller but higher-class market that had existed since 1908 was transformed into a larger market demanding better-class cars for the general public.

In other words, where Ford's goal was providing a cheap mode of transportation, the new market demanded a constantly improving automobile — for everyone.

With the development of the automobile industry in the 1920s, the U.S. economy entered a period of new growth. With it, new elements appeared, further changing the market. These new elements can be divided into four categories:

1. installment payment plan
2. used car trade-ins

3. sedan-type body

4. changing models yearly

If we consider the automobile environment as well, I would add to this list:

5. improved roads

These elements are deeply rooted in today's automobile industry and it is almost impossible to think about the industry without them. Prior to 1920, however, and for a little while after, car buyers were limited to those purchasing a car for the first time; typically they paid in cash or acquired a special loan. Many cars were of the "touring" or "roadster" type, styles that did not change from year to year.

This situation continued for a while. Even if the model changed, the change was not conspicuous until the entire changeover reached completion. New elements developed at different rates and were added separately until, finally, all the changes came together as a completely new model.

Sloan grabbed hold of this important modification in the marketplace and began to offer more and more different models. This "full-line" policy was General Motor's unique strategy to answer public demands. How did the automobile industry as a whole respond to this diversification?[7]

In the transition from mass-produced Model T's to the full-line policy of General Motors, production processes became complicated. To reduce costs while making various types of cars, standard parts had to be developed for use in different models. The Ford system, however, was not modified to any great extent.

At about this time, pricing policies were actively studied and employed in response to the wide variations resulting from diversification in the marketplace. I think that in production, however, the unfinished Ford system changed little and became deeply rooted.

While building up the Toyota production system, I always kept in mind the Japanese market and its demands for many types of cars in small quantities — different from American demands for a few types in large quantities.

The Toyota production system helps production meet market demands. We now know that producing many types of cars in large quantities is economically desirable, even though the Toyota system was built on the premise of many types in small quantities for the Japanese environment. Thus, the system is proving its effectiveness in the mature Japanese market. At the same time, I think the Toyota production system can be applied in America where the market for many types in large quantities has existed since Sloan's time.

▸ Inverse Conception and Business Spirit

Today and Tomorrow was published in America in 1926 at the peak of Henry Ford's career. In fact, this period of time also marked a turning point for the U.S. automobile industry. Later we shall discuss the details of the changes that occurred, but in brief, while the high point in Ford's career, this period ironically marked the beginning of the Ford Company's downward slide and the rise of General Motors.

The year 1926 corresponds to *Taisho 15* in Japan and, coincidentally, was the time when Toyoda Sakichi's auto-activated loom was perfected.

It was Ford who perfected the automobile industry. He knew in detail every material used in his vehicles and his knowledge was not superficial. With his own hands, he created separate business operations for the various metals, including steel and nonferrous metals, and textiles.

Ford thought flexibly about things without getting caught in existing concepts. One of his experiences concerns textiles:

> Spinning and weaving have come down to us through the ages and they have gathered about them traditions which have become almost sacred rules of conduct. The textile industry was one of the first to make use of power, but also it was one of the first to use the labour of children. Many textile manufacturers thoroughly believed that low-cost production is impossible without low-priced

labour. The technical achievements of the industry have been remarkable, but whether it has been possible for anyone to approach the industry with an absolutely open mind, free from tradition, is another matter.[8]

Ford must have written this before the development of Sakichi's auto-activated loom, an invention that changed the textile industry shackled by centuries of tradition. Nonetheless, Ford's ideas and developing business designs open our eyes:

We use more than 100,000 yards of cotton cloth and more than 25,000 yards of woollen cloth during every day of production...

At first, we took for granted that we had to have cotton cloth — we had never used anything but cotton cloth as a foundation material for tops and for artificial leather. We put in a unit of cotton machinery and began to experiment, but, not being bound by tradition, we had not gone far with these experiments before we began to ask ourselves:

Is cotton the best material we can use here?

And we discovered that we had been using cotton cloth, not because it was the best cloth, but because it was the easiest to get. A linen cloth would undoubtedly be stronger, because the strength of cloth depends upon the length of the fibre, and the flax fibre is one of the longest and strongest known. Cotton had to be grown thousands of miles from Detroit. We should have to pay transportation on the raw cotton, if we decided to go into cotton textiles, and we should also have to pay transportation on this cotton converted into motor-car use — very often back again to where it had been grown. Flax can be grown in Michigan and Wisconsin, and we could have a supply at hand practically ready for use. But linen making had even more traditions than cotton, and no one had been able to do much in linen making in this country because of the vast amount of hand labour considered essential.

We began to experiment at Dearborn, and these experiments have demonstrated that flax can be mechanically handled. The work has passed the experimental stage. It has proved its commercial feasibility.[9]

I was intrigued by Ford's question "Is cotton the best material we can use here?"

As Ford pointed out, people follow tradition. This might be acceptable in private life, but in industry, outdated customs must be eliminated. In this process of asking *why*, we see vividly one facet of Ford's business spirit.

Progress cannot be generated when we are satisfied with existing situations. This also applies to improving production methods. If we just walk around aimlessly, we will never be able to ask good questions.

I have always tried to view things upside down. Reading Ford, I was encouraged by the way he repeatedly came up with brilliant inverse conceptions.

► Getting Away from Quantity and Speed

Do not forget that *Today and Tomorrow* was written in the 1920s, over a half century ago when Ford's career was at its peak. Shortly, he would face his first failure and discouragement even though the Ford Motor Company ultimately survived.

As I said earlier, I have long doubted that the mass–production system practiced in America and around the world today, even in Japan, was Ford's true intention. For this reason, I have constantly sought the origin of his ideas. For example, take a look at the American social environment of the 1920s when Ford was prospering:

> But are we moving too fast — not merely in the making of automobiles, but in life generally? One hears a [great] deal about the worker being ground down by hard labour, of what is called progress being made at the expense of something or other, and that efficiency is wrecking all the finer things of life.
>
> It is quite true that life is out of balance — and always has been. Until lately, most people have had no leisure to use and, of course, they do not know how to use it. One of our large problems is to find some balance between work and play, between sleep and food, and eventually to discover why men grow old and die. Of this more later.
>
> Certainly we are moving faster than before. Or, more correctly, we are being moved faster. But is 20 minutes in a motor car

easier or harder than four hours' solid trudging down a dirt road? Which mode of travel leaves the pilgrim fresher at the end? Which leaves him more time and more mental energy? And soon we shall be making an hour by air what were days' journeys by motor. Shall we all then be nervous wrecks?

But does this state of nervous wreckage to which we are all said to be coming exist in life — or in books? One hears of the workers' nervous exhaustion in books, but does one hear of it from the workers? . . .

The very word "efficiency" is hated because so much that is not efficiency has masqueraded as such. Efficiency is merely the doing of work in the best way you know rather than in the worst way. It is the taking of a trunk up a hill on a truck rather than on one's back. It is the training of the worker and the giving to him of power so that he may earn more and have more and live more comfortably. The Chinese coolie working through long hours for a few cents a day is not happier than the American worker with his own home and automobile. The one is a slave, the other is a free man.[10]

There have been many changes in the last half century. Circumstances in China have changed drastically, for instance. Recently, between September 1977 and September 1978, I visited many Chinese industries trying hard to promote modern industrialization.

From Ford's time to the present, through our postwar period when we began work on the Toyota production system, and within the industrialization that China is trying to achieve, there is one universal element — and Ford called it "true efficiency." Ford said efficiency is simply a matter of doing work using the best methods known, not the worst.

The Toyota production system works with the same idea. Efficiency is never a function of quantity and speed. Ford raised the question: "Are we moving too fast?" In connection with the automobile industry, it is undeniable that we have been pursuing efficiency and regarding quantity and speed as its two major factors. The Toyota production system, on the other hand, has always suppressed overproduction, producing in response to the needs of the marketplace.

In the high-growth period, market needs were great and losses caused by overproduction did not appear on the surface. During slow growth, however, excess inventory shows up whether we like it or not. This kind of waste is definitely the result of pursuing quantity and speed.

When describing the characteristics of the Toyota production system, we explained the concept of small lot sizes and quick setup. Actually, at the heart of this is our intention to reform the existing and deeply rooted concept of "faster and more" by generating a continuous work flow.

To be truthful, even at Toyota, it is very difficult to get the die pressing, resin modeling, casting, and forging processes into a total production flow as streamlined as the flows in assembly or machine processing.

For example, with training, setup of a large press can be accomplished in three to five minutes. This is shorter than that of other companies by a surprisingly large margin. In the future, as work flow is perfected, we could slow down and still keep it under 10 minutes.

This explains why the Toyota production system is the opposite of America's system of mass production and quantity sales — the latter system generates unnecessary losses in pursuit of quantity and speed.

6

▼

Surviving the Low-Growth Period

The System Raised in the High-Growth Period

TOWARD THE END of 1955, Japan entered a period of high growth rare for the time in world economics. Kanban, the operating tool of the Toyota production system, was adopted company-wide in 1962, when Japan was well into its growth. It is significant that the kanban system with its roots at Toyota coincided with this period of time.

As soon as Japan entered the high-growth period and courageously called for income doubling, Japan's businessmen seemed to lose sight of traditional Japanese ways. They lost sight of an economy unique to Japanese business, and of the society itself. This "loss of sight" was due to the acceptance of American mass production and the growing public tendency to consider consumption a virtue.

Into the automobile industry came a flood of large, high-performance machines, such as the transfer machine or robot. In a period of high growth, whatever was made was sold, so these mass production machines demonstrated their effectiveness.

However, the problem was one of attitude — of containing and understanding this abundant and rapidly attained economy. At Toyota, although we were excited about automation and robotics, it was very doubtful whether their purpose — a real increase in efficiency — was being achieved.

It is easy to understand the purpose of reducing manpower by using automation and fewer workers with the help of large, high-performance machines. While trying to double income figures, Japan saw national income averages rise sharply and the previous advantage of production costs based on low wages diminish. For these reasons, businesses raced to automate.

However, the machines and equipment used in automation had a serious shortcoming — they were unable to make judgments or stop by themselves. Therefore, to prevent losses caused by damaged machinery, tools, and dies, and the production of large quantities of defective products, supervision by an operator was necessary. Consequently, the number of workers did not decrease with automation. Manual work in most cases just changed names. Thus, while the machines indeed "saved manpower," they did not increase efficiency.

To me, it was questionable whether it was labor-saving when twice the number of workers was needed. It would be all right if we were prepared to reduce the number of workers by half using high-performance machines. But that did not happen. I concluded that the work could be done very well with the existing older equipment.

It is dangerous when industrialists do not realize this. If we blindly followed the trends, what would happen when the economy of scale broke down? It was not difficult to envision the confusion and mayhem that would follow.

Japan's economy expanded in the first two quarters of 1965 and the desire for large, high-performance machines in production plants intensified. This desire was not only at the production level — top management often led the way.

At the time, I seriously felt it would be dangerous to continue purchasing high-performance equipment this way. At Toyota, we all understood this alarming trend, but the problem lay with our affiliates. We gathered their top managers and personally asked them to cooperate, to understand and adopt the Toyota system of production.

We discussed reducing manpower to reduce cost. We even demonstrated from actual Toyota statistics that, by carrying out true rationalization, production could be done more cheaply without robots.

Then and even now, many people harbor these misconceptions. Many think cost reduction can be achieved only if the number of workers is reduced by acquiring robots or high-performance machines. Results show, however, that costs are not reduced at all.

It was obvious that the root of the problem was the idea of labor-saving through automation.

► Raising Productivity During Low Growth

For automation to be effective, we must implement a system in which the machines sense the occurrence of an abnormality and stop themselves. In other words, we must give the automated machines a human touch — enough intelligence to make them autonomated and achieve "worker saving" rather than "labor saving."

The oil crisis in the fall of 1973 brought a new twist to Japan's economy. At Toyota, where production increases had been achieved yearly since the 1930s, we were forced to reduce production for 1974.

Throughout the industrial sector in Japan, profits plummeted as a result of zero growth and the shock of production cutbacks. The results were terrible. At this time, because Toyota had suffered less from the effects of the oil crisis, people began to pay attention to its production system.

With the reduced production that followed the oil crisis, Toyota faced problems that had been hidden or less visible during the previous high-growth period. The problems had to do with the autonomated machines to which a fixed number of operators were assigned.

A perfect autonomated machine, that is, a machine without an operator, was the exception. The autonomated machine that needed two workers to complete a cycle was the problem. With production reduced by 50 percent, the operation still required two workers. One worker was needed at the input and one at the output of a large, autonomated machine, for example.

Thus, an autonomated machine discovers abnormalities and performs the useful role of preventing the production of defective products. From another angle, however, it has the disadvantage of requiring a certain number of workers.

This is a major handicap in any factory that has to respond to a change in production. Therefore, the next step for the Toyota production system was to embark on demolishing the system of a fixed number of workers. This was the concept of reducing the number of workers.

This idea is applied not only to the machine but also to the production line where people are working. A five-worker line, for example, is organized in such a way that the work can be done by four men in case one worker is absent. But the quantity produced is only 80 percent of the standard. To accomplish this, improvements in plant layout and equipment, as well as multi-skilled training of workers must be instituted while times are still normal.

To reduce the number of workers means that a production line or a machine can be operated by one, two, or any number of workers. The idea originated with the need to refute the need for a fixed number of workers for a machine.

Isn't this sort of understanding needed by all businesses during periods of low growth? In a high-growth period, productivity can be raised by anyone. But how many can attain it during the more difficult circumstances induced by low-growth rate? This is the deciding factor in the success or failure of an enterprise.

Even during high growth, to prevent generating excess inventory through overproduction, we avoided arbitrarily buying mass production machinery. We knew how big a strain the approach of "big guns" could be on manufacturing. So we concentrated on developing the Toyota production system without being pushed by the trends.

The Toyota production system first established the basis of rationalization with its production method. Its challenge was the total elimination of waste by using the just-in-time system and kanban.

For every problem, we must have a specific countermeasure. A vague statement that waste should be eliminated, or that there are too many workers, will not convince anybody. But with the introduction of the Toyota production system, waste can be identified immediately and specifically. In fact, I always say production can be done with half as many workers.

At Toyota today, changes are occurring in all production areas. Everyone knows the fluctuations of various factors in producing different types of cars. When one model drops in sales, its costs rise. But you cannot ask the customer to pay more for the car.

Car models in lesser demand still somehow have to be made cheaply and sold for a profit. Facing this fact, we continue to study methods of increasing productivity even when quantities decrease.

Each automobile model has its own history. The Corona currently sells well, but it did not, at first, and we had a difficult time. When a model does not sell well, we must increase efficiency even with small quantities to reduce costs. I always tell people in manufacturing:

"There must be hundreds of people around the world who can improve productivity and efficiency by increasing production quantity. We, too, have such foremen at Toyota. But few people in the world can raise productivity when production quantities decrease. With even one such person, the character of a business operation will be that much stronger."

People prefer working with large quantities, however. It is easier than having to work hard and learn from producing small quantities.

It has been over 30 years since I began work on the Toyota production system. During this period, I have been taught a lot of ideas by many people and by society. Each idea was conceived and developed in response to a need.

I think it is more worthwhile in a company to work in the area where there are problems due to dwindling sales than in an area where sales are rising. The need for improvement is more urgent even though it may not seem that way.

It is a shame that in today's business and industrial society, the relationships between work and worker and machine and worker have become so adversarial. For our development to continue, we must become more generous, more resourceful, and more creative.

As the Toyota production system evolved, I frequently applied reverse common sense or inverse thinking. I urge all managers, intermediate supervisors, foremen, and workers in production to be more flexible in their thinking as they go about their work.

▸ Learning from the Flexibility of Ancient People

Digressing for a moment, it is said that the characters for fermented soybean (*nattō*) and bean curd (*tōfu*) had opposite meanings originally.

There are various theories about this. One holds that Ogyū Sorai, a Confucian scholar of the mid-Edo period, mistook the two terms. Another has it that he intentionally switched them.

Nattō, a product for which the Tōhoku region, Mito, and other areas are famed, should originally have been written the way tofu is now [豆腐], because *nattō* is made by allowing soybeans [豆] to rot [腐].

What we now call "tofu" was originally written with the characters now used for *nattō*, [納豆], because tofu is made from soybeans [豆] and formed [納] into cubes.

The problem is that no one would ever eat *nattō* if the word were written with the characters for "rotten soybeans," while tofu is so white and appetizing that, even if it were written as [腐], no one would think of it as rotten beans. The story goes, then, that each written word was used for the other.

Nomenclature in Japan contains many other fascinating examples of this sort, examples that reveal a characteristically Japanese way of conceiving things.

Among the Chinese characters used in Japanese, we find a thought process in Japanese that differs from the older Chinese. This way of thinking was born in the Japanese environment.

I place value on the native ideas unique to Japan. For instance, although the Toyota Motor Company has become a ¥2 trillion firm, we do not consider moving away from the main office in Mikawa. Sometimes we are warned that by staying in such a place we miss out on the latest news. However, I do not believe this keeps us in the dark information-wise from the world or the rest of Japan. The Toyota-style information system mentioned earlier, organized as part of the Toyota production system, is working very effectively in this sense.

Of course, what is important is not the system but the creativity of human beings who select and interpret the information. Fortunately, the Toyota production system is still being perfected. Improvements are made daily thanks to the vast number of suggestions received from its employees.

My mind has a tendency to crystallize and so I renew my determination every day and force myself to think creatively. There is always much to do in the production field...

Postscript to the Original Japanese Edition

MY WISH HAS been to give readers a basic understanding of the Toyota production system. I wanted to illustrate how it reduces costs by improving productivity with human effort and innovation even in periods of severe low growth — not by increasing quantities.

While writing this book, I witnessed Japanese economy running into more and more serious international problems regarding the yen. This concerns me very much. The automobile industry has grown in the last two or three years primarily through exports. This growth, however, seems to have already reached its limit.

Japanese industry must get away from mass production quickly and make a transition based on bold ideas. It would be very fortunate if the Toyota production system became a useful tool in generating these changes.

Without the assistance of Mr. Mito Setsuo of *Keizai Jānarisuto*, this book would not have been possible. I wish to record the fact here and express my gratitude to him.

I have been renewed and influenced by the writings and personal greatness of Mr. Toyoda Sakichi and Mr. Toyoda Kiichirō. To them I am indebted.

Finally, I wish to thank the staff members of Diamond Inc. for the labor they provided behind the scenes. [Ed. — Diamond is the original Japanese publisher.]

Taiichi Ohno
1978

Glossary of Major Terms

As a guide to understanding and applying the Toyota production system, the author has defined 24 important terms.

▸ Andon

Andon, the line-stop indicator board hung above the production line, is a visual control. The trouble indicator light works as follows:

When operations are normal, the *green light* is on. When a worker wants to adjust something on the line and calls for help, he turns on a *yellow light*. If a line stop is needed to rectify a problem, the *red light* is turned on. To thoroughly eliminate abnormalities, workers should not be afraid to stop the line.

▸ Autonomation (Automation with a Human Touch)

The Toyota production system utilizes *autonomation*, or automation with a human touch, rather than automation. Autonomation means transferring human intelligence to a machine. The concept originated with the auto-activated loom of Toyoda Sakichi. His invention was equipped with a device that automatically and immediately stopped the machine if the vertical or lateral threads broke or ran out. In other words, a device capable of making a judgment was built into the machine.

At Toyota, this concept is applied not only to the machinery but also to the production line and the workers. In other words, if an abnormal situation arises, a worker is required to stop the line. Autonomation prevents the production of defective products, eliminates overproduction, and automatically stops abnormalities on the production line allowing the situation to be investigated.

▸ Baka-Yoke (Fool-Proofing)

To produce quality products 100 percent of the time, innovations must be made to tools and equipment in order to install devices for the prevention of defects. This is called *baka-yoke*, and the following are examples of *baka-yoke* devices:

1. When there is a working mistake, the material will not fit the tool.
2. If there is irregularity in the material, the machine will not start.
3. If there is a working mistake, the machine will not start the machining process.
4. When there are working mistakes or a step left out, corrections are made automatically and machining continues.
5. Irregularities in the earlier process are checked in the later process to stop the defective products.
6. When some step is forgotten, the next process will not start.

▸ Baton Passing Zone

In a swimming relay, the fastest and slowest swimmers must both swim the same fixed distance. In a track relay, however, a faster runner can make up for a slower runner in the baton passing zone. On a production line, the track relay method is preferred. To improve the efficiency of the line, the supervisor must establish a baton passing zone where workers have a chance to catch up.

► Do Not Make Isolated Islands

If workers are isolated here and there, they cannot help each other. But if work combinations are studied and *work distribution*, or work positioning, done to enable workers to assist each other, the number of workers can be reduced. When work flow is properly laid out, small isolated islands do not form.

► Five Why's

The basis of Toyota's scientific approach is to ask *why* five times whenever we find a problem. In the Toyota production system, "5W" means five why's. By repeating *why* five times, the nature of the problem as well as its solution becomes clear. The solution, or the how-to, is designated as "1H." Thus, "Five Why's equal One How" (5W = 1H).

► Just-In-Time

With the possibility of acquiring products at the time and in the quantity needed, waste, unevenness, and unreasonableness can be eliminated and efficiency improved. Toyoda Kiichirō, father of Japanese car manufacturing, originally conceived this idea which his successors then developed into a production system. The thing to remember is that it is not only "in time" but "just in time." *Just-in-time* and *autonomation* constitute the two main pillars of the Toyota production system.

► Kanban

A *kanban* ("tag") is a tool for managing and assuring just-in-time production, the first pillar of the Toyota production system. Basically, a kanban is a simple and direct form of communication always located at the point where it is needed. In most cases, a kanban is a small piece of paper inserted in a rectangular vinyl envelope. On this piece of paper is written how many of what part to pick up or which parts to assemble.

In the just-in-time method, a later process goes to an earlier process to withdraw needed goods, when and in the quantity needed. The earlier process then produces the quantity withdrawn. In this case, when the later process goes to the earlier process to pick up, they are connected by the withdrawal or transport information, called *withdrawal kanban* and *transport kanban*, respectively. This is an important role of kanban.

Another role is the *in-process*, or *production ordering kanban*, which tells the operator to produce the quantity withdrawn from the earlier process. These two kanban work as one, circulating between the processes within the Toyota Motor Company, between the company and its affiliates, and also between the processes in each affiliate.

In addition, there is the *signal kanban* used in the stamping process, for instance, where production of a specific quantity, perhaps more than required by just-in-time, cannot be avoided.

▸ Labor Saving to Worker Saving to Reducing Number of Workers

If large, high-performance machines are bought, we save worker energy. In other words, *labor saving* is achieved. However, it is more important to reduce the number of workers by using these machines and reassigning workers to departments where they are needed. If, as a result of labor saving, 0.9 of a worker is saved, it means nothing. At least one person must be saved before a cost reduction results. Therefore, we must attain *worker saving*.

At Toyota, we set a new goal — to reduce the number of workers. To achieve worker saving, we promoted autonomation. When production was decreased, however, we could not reduce the number of workers proportionately. This was because autonomation was operated by a fixed number of workers. In a low-growth period, we must (1) break down this concept of a fixed number of workers and (2) set up new, flexible production lines where work can be carried on by fewer workers regardless of production quantities. This is the aim of reducing the number of workers.

► Moving vs. Working

Regardless of how much workers move, it does not mean work has been done. *Working* means that progress has been made, that a job is done with little waste and high efficiency. The supervisor must make an effort to turn workers' movements into working.

► Multi-Process Operation System

In the machining process, suppose, for example, that five lathes, five milling machines, and five drilling machines are lined up in two parallel rows. If an operator operates five lathes, we call this a *multi-unit operation system*. The same is true for handling five milling or five drilling machines.

If, however, an operator uses one lathe, one milling machine, and one drilling machine (that is, several processes), we call this a *multi-process operation system*. In the Toyota production system, setting up the production flow is of primary importance. Therefore, we try to achieve a multi-process operation system that directly reduces the number of workers. For the worker on the production line, this means shifting from being *single-skilled* to becoming *multi-skilled*.

► Operating Rate and Operable Rate

The *operating rate* is the current production level in relation to the full operating capacity of the machine for a specific length of time. If sales go down, the operating rate naturally drops. On the other hand, if orders increase, the operating rate can reach 120 percent or more through shift work or overtime. Whether an operating rate is good or bad is determined by the way equipment is used relative to the quantity of products needed.

The *operable rate* at Toyota means the machine's availability and operable condition when operation is desired. The ideal 100 percent depends on good equipment maintenance and rapid changeovers.

▸ Production Leveling

On a production line, fluctuations in product flow increase waste. This is because the equipment, workers, inventory, and other elements required for production must always be prepared for peak production. If a later process varies its withdrawal of parts in terms of timing and quantity, the range of these fluctuations will increase as they move up the line toward the earlier processes.

To prevent fluctuations in production even in outside affiliates, we must try to keep fluctuation in the final assembly line to zero. Toyota's final assembly line never assembles the same automobile model in a batch. Production is *leveled* by making first one model, then another model, then yet another.

▸ Profit-Making Industrial Engineering

The production management technique we call industrial engineering (IE) came from America. Traditional definitions aside, in the Toyota production system, IE is regarded as the production technology that attempts to reduce costs by harmonizing quality, quantity, and timing throughout the production area. It is not the IE method discussed in academia. The most important characteristic of Toyota-style IE is that it is a *profit-earning IE* tied directly to cost reduction.

▸ Real Cause

Underneath the "cause" of a problem, the *real cause* is hidden. In every case, we must dig up the real cause by asking *why*,

why, why, why, why. Otherwise, countermeasures cannot be taken and problems will not be truly solved.

► Required Numbers Equal Production Quantity

At Toyota, production quantity equals market demand or actual orders. In other words, the number needed is the number sold. Therefore, because market needs are directly connected to production, manufacturing cannot arbitrarily change production quantities. To reduce overproduction, efficiency improvement must be achieved on the basis of *required numbers*. In other words, production quantities are based on demand.

► Small Lot Sizes and Quick Setups

In production leveling, batches are made as small as possible in contrast to traditional mass production, where bigger is considered better. At Toyota we try to avoid assembling the same type of car in batches. Of course, when the final assembly process does produce this way, the earlier process — such as the press operation — naturally has to go along with it. This means die changes must be done frequently. Up to now, conventional wisdom has dictated having each die press punch out as many parts as possible. In the Toyota production system, however, this does not apply. Die changes are made quickly and improved even more with practice. In the 1940s, it took two to three hours. In the 1950s, it dropped from one hour to 15 minutes. Presently, setups have been shortened to three minutes.

► Standard Work Procedures

For just-in-time production to be carried out, standard work sheets for each process must be clear and concise. The three elements of a standard work sheet are:

1. *Cycle time*, the length of time (minutes and seconds) in which one unit is to be made;
2. *Work sequence*, the sequence of work in the flow of time;
3. *Standard inventory*, the minimum amount of goods needed to keep the process going.

▸ Stopping the Line

A production line that does not stop is either a perfect line or a line with big problems. When many people are assigned to a line and the flow does not stop, it means problems are not surfacing. This is bad.

It is important to set up a line so that it can be stopped when necessary:

• to prevent generating defective products,
• to make improvements with only a few workers, and finally,
• to develop a line that is strong and rarely needs to be stopped.

There is no reason to fear a line stop.

▸ Toyota Production System

The first aspect of the Toyota production system is the *Toyota-style method of production*, which means putting a *flow* into the manufacturing process. In the past, lathes were located in the lathe area, and milling machines in the milling area. Now, we place a lathe, a milling machine, and a drilling machine in the actual sequence of the manufacturing processing.

This way, instead of having one worker per machine, one worker oversees many machines or, more accurately, *one worker operates many processes*. This improves productivity.

Next is the *kanban* system, an operational tool that carries out the *just-in-time* production method. Kanban assures that the right parts are available at the time and in the quantity needed by functioning as the withdrawal or transport information, an order for conveyance or delivery of the goods and also as a *work order* within the production processes.

► Visual Control (Management by Sight)

Autonomation means stopping the production line or the machine whenever an abnormal situation arises. This clarifies what is normal and what is abnormal. In terms of quality, any defective products are forced to surface because the actual progress of work in comparison to daily production plans is always clearly visible. This idea applies to machines and the line as well as to the arrangement of goods and tools, inventory, circulation of kanban, standard work procedures, and so on. In production lines using the Toyota production system, *visual control*, or *management by sight*, is enforced.

► Waste Recognition and Elimination

To recognize waste, we must understand its nature. Production waste can be divided into the following categories:

- overproduction
- waiting
- transporting
- too much machining (over-processing)
- inventories
- moving
- making defective parts and products

Consider the waste of overproduction, for example. It is not an exaggeration to say that in a low-growth period such waste is a crime against society more than a business loss. Eliminating waste must be a business's first objective.

▸ Work Flow and Work Forced to Flow

Work flow means that value is added to the product in each process while the product flows along. If goods are carried by conveyor, this is not work flow, but work forced to flow. The basic achievement of the Toyota production system is setting up the manufacturing flow. This naturally means establishing a work flow.

▸ Work Improvement vs. Equipment Improvement

Plans to improve production can be roughly divided into (1) *work improvement*, such as establishing work standards, redistributing work, and clearly indicating the places where things are to be placed, and (2) *equipment improvement*, such as buying equipment and making machines autonomated. Equipment improvement takes money and cannot be undone.

In the Toyota production system, sequencing of work and work standardization are done first. In this way, most problem areas can be eliminated or improved. If equipment improvement comes first, manufacturing processes will never be improved.

Editor's Notes

Chapter 1

1. For comparative statistics between Japanese and U.S. auto makers, see pages 215-217 in Michael A. Cusumano's *The Japanese Automobile Industry* (The Council on East Asian Studies, Harvard University, distributed by Harvard University Press, 1985).

2. In 1937, Toyota Motor Company was founded by Toyoda Kiichirō, the son of Toyoda Sakichi, an automatic loom inventor fascinated by motor vehicles and founder of Toyoda Spinning and Weaving and Toyoda Automatic Loom. The family name "Toyoda," which means "abundant rice field," was changed to "Toyota" by the automobile division for marketing purposes. The word is an alternate reading of the two logographs with which the family name is written. [Ibid., 59.]

Chapter 2

1. Maruzen is a chain of Japanese bookstores.

2. There are three distinct regional markets in Japan: Kantō, encompassing the Tokyo area; Kansai, in the Kyoto-Osaka region; and Nagoya, wherein lies Toyota City. Each region personifies different business qualities. [David J. Lu, *Inside Corporate Japan* (Cambridge, MA: Productivity Press, 1987), Ch. 1.]

3. The term "rationalization" is frequently used in Japanese writings to indicate activities undertaken to upgrade technology, improve quality, and reduce cost. It may also mean reorganizing and integrating an industry while engaged in the above-mentioned activities. [Ibid., 227.]

Chapter 3

1. From *Factory* magazine, formerly published by McGraw-Hill and defunct since 1977.

2. Attributed to Professor W.V. Clark, Massachusetts Institute of Technology, who met with the inspection party of Japan's IE Association founded by the Japan Productivity Center for the purpose of studying American IE in the early 1960s. The IE definition attributed to Professor Clark is not in his original words but has been retranslated into English from Japanese.

3. This IE definition is an English translation of a Japanese translation of the original English definition. The source of the original English definition cannot be located.

Chapter 4

1. Toyoda Eiji was president of Toyota Motor Company from 1967 to 1982. Born in 1913, he was the cousin of Toyoda Kiichirō and the son of Toyoda Sakichi's brother.

2. Taka-Diastase is the trade name of a digestive compound developed by Dr. Takamine Jōkichi (1854-1922), a Japanese chemist who worked in the United States. Takamine was also the first to succeed in the extraction of epinephrine.

3. Dr. Noguchi Hideyo (1876-1928) was a Japanese-born American physician and bacteriologist who worked in the United States.

4. An earthquake in 1923 in the Tokyo area prompted the municipal government to import thousands of Model T trucks from the United States to replace destroyed transportation networks and to distribute supplies. [Cusumano, op. cit., 17.]

5. Honda Kōtarō was a professor at Tōhoku University and Japan's leading expert in iron alloys.

6. This 1936 legislation, drafted by the military, required that companies making over 3,000 vehicles per year obtain a license from the government. Only firms with over 50 percent of their shares and members of their board of directors held by Japanese citizens could be licensed. [Ibid., 17.]

Chapter 5

1. Charles E. Sorensen, with Samuel T. Williamson, *My Forty Years with Ford* (New York: W.W. Norton & Company, 1956), 117-118.

2. *Today and Tomorrow* has been out of print for decades. Because of its educational value, Productivity Press will issue a commemorative edition in 1988.

3. Henry Ford, *Today and Tomorrow* (New York: Doubleday and Company, 1926), 90-92.

4. Ibid., 78.

5. Ibid., 79.

6. Ibid., 192.

7. While Ford had always produced just one car type, General Motors in 1923 began offering several car types with yearly model changes. [Cusumano, op. cit., 270.]

8. Ford, op. cit., 55-56.

9. Ibid., 56-57.

10. Ibid., 4-6.

About the Author

TAIICHI OHNO WAS born in Dairen (Port Arthur), Man-churia, China, in February 1912. In 1932, after graduating from the department of mechanical engineering, Nagoya Technical High School, he joined Toyoda Spinning and Weaving. In 1943, he was transferred to the Toyota Motor Company where he was named machine shop manager in 1949. He became Toyota's director in 1954, managing direc-tor in 1964, senior managing director in 1970, and executive vice president in 1975. Although he retired from Toyota in 1978, Mr. Ohno continues as chairman of Toyoda Spinning and Weaving. He resides in Toyota-shi, Aichi-ken.

This book first appeared in Japan in May 1978 and reached its twentieth printing in February 1980. Productivity Press's 1988 edition is the first printed for the English-reading public.

Index

American technology
  catching up with the
    techniques, 3
  production system, 1
  single-skilled operator, 14
  work forces, ratio between
    Japanese and, 3
Andon (the line stop
  indication board), 21, 121
Apparent increase of efficiency
  See Efficiency
Assembly, final line, 5, 34, 42
Automobile industry in Japan
  assembly line, 49
  compared with America, 3
  difficulty developing the, 84
  history of, 76
  manufacturing,
    major problem in, 81
  number of processes involved, 4
  production flow, 5
Autonomation, 6-8, 45-46
  See also Toyota
    production system
  definition of, 6, 121
  dual role of, 8
  equipment improvement, 67
  extraordinary character of, 77-78
  machine safety devices, 6

Autonomation (cont.)
  visual control, 8

Baka-yoke (fool-proofing), 6, 122
Balance weights,
  five types of, 43-44
Baton-passing system (zone), 122
  See also "Mutual Assistance
    Campaign"; Work arena
Book value
  See Equipment, value of old
Business organization,
  like the human body, 45
  reflexes, 46-47

Capacity
  generating excess, 56-57
  present, formula for, 19
  line
    See Line capacity
Carinas, 96
CIM, x
Comparative statistics
  between Japanese and U.S.
    automakers, 131
Competition
  legislation to prevent wild, 86
  with the U.S. and Europe, xiii
  within Japan, 23

137

Mura (inconsistency), 41
Muri (unreasonableness), 41
"Mutual Assistance Campaign," 25

Ninjutsu, management by, 68-70
NKS magnet, 90
Non-value-added wastes.
   See Wastes
Non-value-added work, 57
Notes, editor's
   See Editor's notes

Ohno, Mr. Taiichi, ix to xii
   about the author, 135
   developer of Toyota production
      system xviii
      See also Toyota
         production system
Oil crisis, 1973, 1-2
Operable rate, 60, 126
Operable time, 60
Operating rate, 60, 125
Overproduction, 43, 59, 62, 66, 108
   See also Manpower, reducing

Plant-first principle, my, 20-21
Price of automobile, economical,
   86-87
      See also Products, making value
Problems, uncovering root, 17
   See also Why, asking, five times
Production
   fine adjustments to, 51
   Japanese-style, 84-85
   line, strong, meaning of,
      102, 128
   management, 4
   monthly schedules, 48
   plant, 20
   schedule, eliminating, 31
Production flow
   establishing a, 11-12
   rearranging the machines, 14
Production leveling, 12-13, 27,

Production leveling (cont.)
   33, 37, 126
   and marketing diversification,
      39-40
   challenge to, 38-39
Production system
   See Also Just-in-time;
      Pull method; Push method;
      Toyota production system
   conventional American mass, 1
   Toyota
      See Toyota production system
Products, making value, 85-89
Pull method, xiv
   definition, xvii
Push method, xiv
   definition, xvii

QC (quality control)
   See Management techniques
Quantity required per day, 22
Quick setup
   See Setup, small lots and quick

Rapid changeovers, 96
Rationalization, 131
Reducing manpower
   See Manpower, reducing
Removing non-value-added waste
   See Wastes
Replace old machinery, decision to
   See Equipment, value of old
Required numbers, 61, 127
Residual value
   See Equipment, value of old
Robotics, x

Safety on the job
   See Autonomation
Setup, small lots and quick, 95-97
Sloan, Alfred P., Jr.
   See General Motors,
      My Years with General Motors

Books from Productivity, Inc.

Productivity, Inc. publishes books that empower individuals and companies to achieve excellence in quality, productivity, and the creative involvement of all employees. Through steadfast efforts to support the vision and strategy of continuous improvement, Productivity Press delivers today's leading-edge tools and techniques gathered directly from industry leaders around the world. Call toll-free 1-800-394-6868 for our free catalog.

5 Pillars of the Visual Workplace
The Sourcebook for 5S Implementation
Hiroyuki Hirano

In this important sourcebook, JIT expert Hiroyuki Hirano provides the most vital information available on the visual workplace. He describes the 5S's: in Japanese they are seiri, seiton, seiso, seiketsu, and shitsuke (which translate as sort, set in order, shine, standardize, and sustain). Hirano discusses how the 5S theory fosters efficiency, maintenance, and continuous improvement in all areas of the company, from the plant floor to the sales office. This book includes case material, graphic illustrations, and photographs.
ISBN 1-56327-047-1 / 377 pages, illustrated / $85.00 / Order FIVE-B163

20 Keys to Workplace Improvement (Revised Edition)
Iwao Kobayashi

The 20 Keys system does more than just bring together twenty of the world's top manufacturing improvement approaches—it integrates these individual methods into a closely interrelated system for revolutionizing every aspect of your manufacturing organization. This revised edition of Kobayashi's bestseller amplifies the synergistic power of raising the levels of all these critical areas simultaneously. The new edition presents upgraded criteria for the five-level scoring system in most of the 20 Keys, supporting your progress toward becoming not only best in your industry but best in the world.
ISBN 1-56327-109-5 / 302 pages / $50.00 / Order 20KREV-B163

PRODUCTIVITY, INC., DEPT. BK, P.O. BOX 13390, PORTLAND, OR 97213-0390
Telephone: 1-800-394-6868   Fax: 1-800-394-6286

Becoming Lean
Inside Stories of U.S. Manufacturers
Jeffrey Liker

Most other books on lean management focus on technical methods and offer a picture of what a lean system should look like. Some provide snapshots of before and after. This is the first book to provide technical descriptions of successful solutions and performance improvements. The first book to include powerful first-hand accounts of the complete process of change, its impact on the entire organization, and the rewards and benefits of becoming lean. At the heart of this book you will find the stories of American manufacturers who have successfully implemented lean methods. Authors offer personalized accounts of their organization's lean transformation, including struggles and successes, frustrations and surprises. Now you have a unique opportunity to go inside their implementation process to see what worked, what didn't, and why. Many of these executives and managers who led the charge to becoming lean in their organizations tell their stories here for the first time!
ISBN 1-56327-173-7/ 350 pages / $35.00 / Order LEAN-B163

Fast Track to Waste-Free Manufacturing
Straight Talk from a Plant Manager
John W. Davis

Batch, or mass, manufacturing is still the preferred system of production for most U.S.-based industry. But to survive, let alone become globally competitive, companies will have to put aside their old habitual mass manufacturing paradigms and completely change their existing system of production. In *Fast Track to Waste-Free Manufacturing: Straight Talk from a Plant Manager*, John Davis details a new and proven system called Waste-Free Manufacturing (WFM) that rapidly deploys the lean process. He covers nearly every aspect of the lean revolution and provides essential tools and techniques you will need to implement WFM. Drawing from more than 30 years of manufacturing experience, John Davis gives you tools and techniques for eliminating anything that cannot be clearly established as value added.
ISBN: 1-56327-212-1 / 425 pages / $45.00 / Order WFM-B163

Implementing TPM
The North American Experience
Charles J. Robinson and Andrew P. Ginder

The authors document an approach to TPM planning and deployment that modifies the JIPM 12-step proc-ess to accommodate the experiences of North American plants. They include details and advice on specific deployment steps, OEE calculation methodology, and autonomous maintenance deployment. This book shows how to make TPM work in unionized plants and how to position TPM to support and complement other strategic manufacturing improvement initiatives.
ISBN 1-56327-087-0 / 224 pages / $45.00 / Order IMPTPM-B163

PRODUCTIVITY, INC., DEPT. BK, P.O. BOX 13390, PORTLAND, OR 97213-0390
Telephone: 1-800-394-6868   Fax: 1-800-394-6286

Integrating Kanban with MRPII
Automating a Pull System for Enhanced JIT Inventory Management
Raymond S. Louis

Manufacturing organizations continuously strive to match the supply of products to market demand. Now for the first time, the automated kanban system is introduced utilizing MRPII. This book describes an automated kanban system that integrates MRPII, kanban bar codes and a simple version of electronic data interchange into a breakthrough system that substantially lowers inventory and significantly eliminates non-value adding activities. This new system automatically recalculates and triggers replenishment, integrates suppliers into the manufacturing loop, and uses bar codes to enhance speed and accuracy of the receipt process. From this book, you will learn how to enhance the flexibility of your manufacturing organization and dramatically improve your competitive position.
ISBN 1-56327-182-6 / 200 pages / $45.00 / Order INTKAN-B163

Kaizen for Quick Changeover
Going Beyond SMED
Kenichi Sekine and Keisuke Arai

Especially useful for manufacturing managers and engineers, this book describes exactly how to achieve faster changeover. Picking up where Shingo's SMED book left off, you'll learn how to streamline the process even further to reduce changeover time and optimize staffing at the same time.
ISBN 0-915299-38-0 / 315 pages / $75.00 / Order KAIZEN-B163

Kanban and Just-In-Time at Toyota
Management Begins at the Workplace
Japan Management Association / Translated by David J. Lu

Toyota's world-renowned success proves that with kanban, the Just-In-Time production system (JIT) makes most other manufacturing practices obsolete. This simple but powerful classic is based on seminars given by JIT creator Taiichi Ohno to introduce Toyota's own supplier companies to JIT. It shows how to implement the world's most efficient production system. A clear and complete introduction.
ISBN 0-915299-48-8 / 211 pages / $40.00 / Order KAN-B163

One-Piece Flow
Cell Design for Transforming the Production Process
Kenichi Sekine

By reconfiguring your traditional assembly lines into production cells based on one-piece flow, you can drastically reduce your lead time, staffing requirements, and number of defects. Sekine examines the basic principles of process flow building, then offers detailed case studies of how various industries designed unique one-piece flow systems to meet their particular needs.
ISBN 0-915299-33-X / 308 pages / $75.00 / Order 1PIECE-B163

PRODUCTIVITY, INC., DEPT. BK, P.O. BOX 13390, PORTLAND, OR 97213-0390
Telephone: 1-800-394-6868   Fax: 1-800-394-6286

P-M Analysis
An Advanced Step in TPM Implementation
Kunio Shirose, Yoshifumi Kimura, and Mitsugu Kaneda

P-M analysis is an effective methodology to find and control the causes of equipment-related chronic losses. Chronic loss stems from complex and interrelated causes, and in most cases, it is very difficult to understand how any single cause impacts the overall problem. P-M Analysis is used to overcome the weaknesses of traditional improvement activities in addressing these losses. This well-illustrated book uses thorough discussion, case studies of implementation, and provides a disciplined step-by-step approach to identify and eliminate causes of chronic equipment-related loss.
ISBN 1-56327-035-8 / 198 pages / $65.00 / Order PMA-B163

Poka-Yoke
Improving Product Quality by Preventing Defects
Nikkan Kogyo Shimbun Ltd. and Factory Magazine (ed.)

If your goal is 100 percent zero defects, here is the book for you—a completely illustrated guide to poka-yoke (mistake-proofing) for supervisors and shopfloor workers. Many poka-yoke devices come from line workers and are implemented with the help of engineering staff. The result is better product quality—and greater participation by workers in efforts to improve your processes, your products, and your company as a whole.
ISBN 0-915299-31-3 / 295 pages / $65.00 / Order IPOKA-B163

Quick Response Manufacturing
A Companywide Approach to Reducing Lead Times
Rajan Suri

Quick Response Manufacturing (QRM) is an expansion of time-based competition (TBC) strategies which use speed for a competitive advantage. Essentially, QRM stems from a single principle: to reduce lead times. But unlike other time-based competition strategies, QRM is an approach for the entire organization, from the front desk to the shop floor, from purchasing to sales. In order to truly succeed with speed-based competition, you must adopt the approach throughout the organization.
ISBN 1-56327-201-6/ 560 pages / $50.00 / Order QRM-B163

A Revolution in Manufacturing
The SMED System
Shigeo Shingo

The heart of JIT is quick changeover methods. Dr. Shingo, inventor of the Single-Minute Exchange of Die (SMED) system for Toyota, shows you how to reduce your changeovers by an average of 98 percent! By applying Shingo's techniques, you'll see rapid improvements (lead time reduced from weeks to days, lower inventory and warehousing costs) that will improve quality, productivity, and profits.
ISBN 0-915299-03-8 / 383 pages / $75.00 / Order SMED-B163

PRODUCTIVITY, INC., DEPT. BK, P.O. BOX 13390, PORTLAND, OR 97213-0390
Telephone: 1-800-394-6868   Fax: 1-800-394-6286

TPM in Process Industries

Tokutaro Suzuki (ed.)

Process industries have a particularly urgent need for collaborative equipment management systems like TPM that can absolutely guarantee safe, stable operation. In *TPM in Process Industries,* top consultants from JIPM (Japan Institute of Plant Maintenance) document approaches to implementing TPM in process industries. They focus on the process environment and equipment issues such as process loss structure and calculation, autonomous maintenance, equipment and process improvement, and quality maintenance. Must reading for any manager in the process industry.

ISBN 1-56327-036-6 / 400 pages / $85.00 / Order TPMPI-B163

Uptime
Strategies for Excellence in Maintenance Management

John Dixon Campbell

Campbell outlines a blueprint for a world class maintenance program by examining, piece by piece, its essential elements—leadership (strategy and management), control (data management, measures, tactics, planning and scheduling), continuous improvement (RCM and TPM), and quantum leaps (process reengineering). He explains each element in detail, using simple language and practical examples from a side range of industries. This book is for every manager who needs to see the "big picture" of maintenance management. In addition to maintenance, engineering, and manufacturing managers, all business managers will benefit from this comprehensive yet realistic approach to improving asset performance.

ISBN 1-56327-053-6 / 180 pages / $35.00 / Order UP-B163

Zero Quality Control
Source Inspection and the Poka-Yoke System

Shigeo Shingo

Dr. Shingo reveals his unique defect prevention system, which combines source inspection and poka-yoke (mistake-proofing) devices that provide instant feedback on errors before they can become defects. The result: 100 percent inspection that eliminates the need for SQC and produces defect-free products without fail. Includes 112 examples, most costing under $100. Two-part video program also available; call for details.

ISBN 0-915299-07-0 / 328 pages / $75.00 / Order ZQC-B163

PRODUCTIVITY, INC., DEPT. BK, P.O. BOX 13390, PORTLAND, OR 97213-0390
Telephone: 1-800-394-6868   Fax: 1-800-394-6286

TO ORDER: Write, phone, or fax Productivity, Inc., Dept. BK, P.O. Box 13390, Portland, OR 97213-0390, phone 1-800-394-6868, fax 1-800-394-6286. Send check or charge to your credit card (American Express, Visa, MasterCard accepted).

U.S. ORDERS: Add $5 shipping for first book, $2 each additional for UPS surface delivery. Add $5 for each AV program containing 1 or 2 tapes; add $12 for each AV program containing 3 or more tapes. We offer attractive quantity discounts for bulk purchases of individual titles; call for more information.

ORDER BY E-MAIL: Order 24 hours a day from anywhere in the world. Use either address:
To order: service@productivityinc.com
To view the online catalog and/or order: http://www.productivityinc.com

QUANTITY DISCOUNTS: For information on quantity discounts, please contact our sales department.

INTERNATIONAL ORDERS: Write, phone, or fax for quote and indicate shipping method desired. For international callers, telephone number is 503-235-0600 and fax number is 503-235-0909. Prepayment in U.S. dollars must accompany your order (checks must be drawn on U.S. banks). When quote is returned with payment, your order will be shipped promptly by the method requested.

Note: Prices are in U.S. dollars and are subject to change without notice.

About the Shopfloor Series

Put powerful and proven improvement tools in the hands of your entire workforce!

Progressive shopfloor improvement techniques are imperative for manufacturers who want to stay competitive and to achieve world class excellence. And it's the comprehensive education of all shopfloor workers that ensures full participation and success when implementing new programs. The Shopfloor Series books make practical information accessible to everyone by presenting major concepts and tools in simple, clear language and at a reading level that has been adjusted for operators by skilled instructional designers. One main idea is presented every two to four pages so that the book can be picked up and put down easily. Each chapter begins with an overview and ends with a summary section. Helpful illustrations are used throughout.

Books currently in the Shopfloor Series include:

5S for Operators
5 Pillars of the Visual Workplace
The Productivity Development Team
ISBN 1-56327-123-0 / 133 pages
Order 5SOP-B163 / $25.00

Mistake-Proofing for Operators
The Productivity Development Team
ISBN 1-56327-127-3 / 93 pages
Order ZQCOP-B163 / $25.00

TPM for Supervisors
The Productivity Development Team
ISBN 1-56327-161-3 / 96 pages
Order TPMSUP-B163 / $25.00

Cellular Manufacturing
The Productivity Development Team
ISBN 1-56327-213-X / 96 pages
Order CELL-B163 / $25.00

Just-In-Time for Operators
The Productivity Development Team
ISBN 1-56327-133-8 / 84 pages
Order JITOP-B163 / $25.00

OEE for Operators
The Productivity Development Team
ISBN 1-56327-221-0 / 96 pages
Order OEEOP-B163 / $25.00

Quick Changeover for Operators
The SMED System
The Productivity Development Team
ISBN 1-56327-125-7 / 93 pages
Order QCOOP-B163 / $25.00

TPM Team Guide
Kunio Shirose
ISBN 1-56327-079-X / 175 pages
Order TGUIDE-B163 / $25.00

TPM for Every Operator
Japan Institute of Plant Maintenance
ISBN 1-56327-080-3 / 136 pages
Order TPMEO-B163 / $25.00

Autonomous Maintenance
Japan Institute of Plant Maintenance
ISBN 1-56327-082-X / 138 pages
Order AUTMOP-B163 / $25.00

Focused Equipment
Improvement
Japan Institute of Plant Maintenance
ISBN 1-56327-081-1 / 138 pages
Order FEIOP-B163 / $25.00

1945

1949 ▶ ——————————————— **1958 ▶**
Intermediate warehouses abolished
Warehouse
withdrawal slip
abolished

1950 ▶ ——————— **1955 ▶**
Machining and assembly   Assembly and body
lines synchronized   plants linked

1948 ▶ ——————————— **1953 ▶**
Withdrawal by subsequent   Supermarket system
processes ("upstream" transport)   in machine shop

1955 ▶ ———————————
Required number system adopted
for supplied parts

1953 ▶ ———————————
Call system for
the machine shop

1955 ▶
Whirligig water system
(small load / mixed transportation)

HISTORY

OF THE

TOYOTA

PRODUCTION

SYSTEM

1945-55 ▶ ———————————————
Setups (2 to 3 hours)

1957 ▶ ———————
Procedural chart
(*andon*) adopted

1947 ▶ ——————— **1949-50 ▶** ———————————
2-machine handling   3- or 4-machine handling (horseshoe)
(parallel or in   or rectangular layout)
L-shaped layout)

Separation of machine work and worker's work begins

1950 ▶ ——————— **1955 ▶** ———————————
Visual control, *andon*   Main plant assembly line production system
system adopted in   (*andon*, line stop, mixed load)
engine assembly   (automation ⟶ autonomation)

1953 ▶   P   R

1945

1961 ▶ ——————— (Ended in failure)
Pallet kanban

1962 ▶
Kanban adopted company-wide
(machining, forging, body assembly, etc.)

1961 ▶ ——————— 1965 ▶
Red and blue card system   Kanban adopted for ordering
for ordering outside parts   outside parts, 100% supply system;
                                  began teaching Toyota system to affiliates

1959 ▶ ——————————————— 1973 ▶
Transfer system (in ⟶ in or in ⟶ out)   Transfer system
                                           (out ⟶ in)

1962 ▶ ——————— 1971 ▶
Main plant setups (15 minutes)   Main office and
                                  Motomachi setups
                                  (3 minutes)

1963 ▶ ——————— 1971 ▶
Use of inter-writer; system   Body indication system
of autonomated selection of   (Motomachi Crown line)
parts adopted; information
indicator system adopted

1963 ▶
Multi-process operation

1962 ▶ ——————— 1966 ▶
Full-work control of machines,   First autonomated line,
machine *baka-yoke*   Kamigō plant

1961 ▶ ——————— 1971 ▶
Andon installed, Motomachi assembly plant   Fixed-position stopping
                                                system in assembly

D U C T I O N   L E V E L I N G

1945

JUST-IN-TIME

1949 ► ———————————————————— **1958 ►**
Intermediate warehouses abolished
Warehouse
withdrawal slip
abolished

1950 ► ———————— **1955 ►**
Machining and assembly   Assembly and body
lines synchronized   plants linked

1948 ► ———————— **1953 ►**
Withdrawal by subsequent   Supermarket system
processes ("upstream" transport)   in machine shop

HISTORY
OF THE
TOYOTA
PRODUCTION
SYSTEM

1955 ► ——————————————
Required number system adopted
for supplied parts

1953 ► ——————————————
Call system for
the machine shop

1955 ►
Whirligig water system
(small load / mixed transportation)

1945-55 ► ———————————————————————
Setups (2 to 3 hours)

1957 ► ————
Procedural chart
(*andon*) adopted

1947 ► ———————— **1949-50 ►** ——————————————
2-machine handling   3- or 4-machine handling (horseshoe)
(parallel or in   or rectangular layout)
L-shaped layout)

Separation of machine work and worker's work begins

1950 ► ———————— **1955 ►** ——————————————
Visual control, *andon*   Main plant assembly line production system
system adopted in   (*andon*, line stop, mixed load)
engine assembly   (automation ⟶ autonomation)

1953 ►   P   R

AUTONOMATION

1945 ———————————————————————————